BULGARIA

MACEDONIA

ISTANBUL

ALBANIA

40°N

SAMOTHRÁKI

ÇANAKKALE

TROY

ORFU

GREECE

TURKEY

ÉVVOIA

SKÍROS

ITHACA

ATHENS

ÁNDROS

KUŞADASI

KEFALLINÍA

TÍNOS

PELOPÓNNISOS

DELOS

IONIAN
SEA

RODOS

CAPE MALEA

KITHIRA

CRETE

M E D I T E R R A N E A N
S E A

LIBYA

24° E

32°N

DRA

BANGHAZI

WE FOLLOWED
ODYSSEUS

To Jane Zimmer

Hal Roth
Margaret Roth

BOOKS BY HAL ROTH

Pathway in the Sky

Two on a Big Ocean

After 50,000 Miles

Two Against Cape Horn

The Longest Race

Always a Distant Anchorage

Chasing the Long Rainbow

Chasing the Wind

We Followed Odysseus

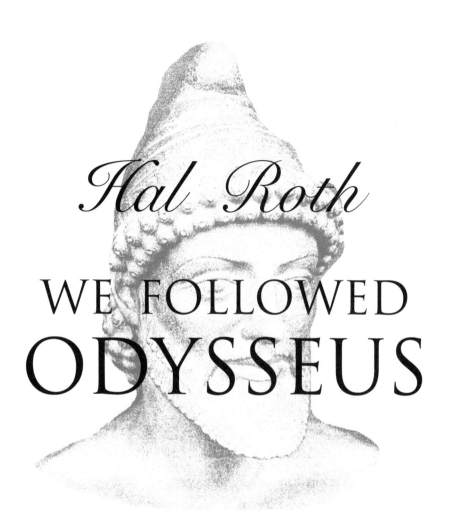

Hal Roth

WE FOLLOWED
ODYSSEUS

PHOTOGRAPHS BY HAL ROTH

SEAWORTHY PUBLICATIONS, INC.
Port Washington, Wisconsin

Seaworthy Publications, Inc.
507 Sunrise Drive
Port Washington, Wisconsin 53074
PHONE: 414-268-9250
FAX: 414-268-9208
E-MAIL: publisher@seaworthy.com

On the World Wide Web at:
www.seaworthy.com

Please contact us for a copy of our catalog.

Cover design by Jack W. Davis.
Text design and composition by John Reinhardt Book Design.

Printed in the United States of America on acid-free paper.

Library of Congress Cataloging in Publication Data

Roth, Hal, 1927–
  We followed Odysseus / by Hal Roth.
     p.   cm.
  Includes bibliographical references and index.
  ISBN 1-892399-03-2 (alk. paper)
  1. Homer. Odyssey. 2. Roth, Hal, 1927– —Journeys-Aegean Islands (Greece and Turkey) 3. Roth, Hal, 1927– —Journeys-Mediterranean Region. 4. Geographical myths in literature. 5. Voyages and travels-Mythology. 6. Homer-Knowledge-Geography. 7. Odysseus (Greek mythology) 8. Classical geography. 9. Voyages and travels. 10. Ships, Ancient. I. Title.
PA41670.R69 1999
883'.01—dc21   98-56146
                                                      CIP

CONTENTS

CONTENTS

MAPS

ACKNOWLEDGMENTS

The publisher and author gratefully acknowledge permission from:

WORDSWORTH EDITIONS of Ware, Hertfordshire, England for eleven lines from *The Odyssey* (1932) translated by T. E. Lawrence.

THE VIKING PRESS of New York for eleven lines from *The Iliad* by Homer, translated by Robert Fagles. Translation ©1990 by Robert Fagles. Introduction and Notes ©1990 by Bernard Knox. Used by permission of Viking Penguin, a division of Penguin Putnam, Inc.

THE VIKING PRESS of New York for seven lines from *The Odyssey* by Homer, translated by Robert Fagles. Translation ©1996 by Robert Fagles. Used by permission of Viking Penguin, a division of Penguin Putnam Inc.

PENGUIN BOOKS of Harmondsworth, Middlesex, England for twenty-three lines from *The Odyssey* (1946) translated by E. V. Rieu.

W. W. NORTON of New York for eight lines from *The Odyssey* (1967) translated by Albert Cook.

HODDER AND STOUGHTON of London for four lines from *Ulysses Found* (1963) by Ernle Bradford.

POLYCTOR TOURS of Piraeus, Greece for permission to use the photograph of the Odysseus statue. Thanks to the GNTO and Eve Tsirigotakis.

THE DEPARTMENT OF SPECIAL COLLECTIONS OF THE NIMITZ LIBRARY at the U.S. Naval Academy in Annapolis, Maryland for two drawings from early nineteenth-century British Pilot books.

DR. SARANTIS SYMEONOGLOU for the use of his photograph of Mt. Aetos.

THE BENAKI MUSEUM OF ATHENS for the vase on page 5. Inv. No. 28187.

ILLUSTRATIONS

PREFACE

WHEN I BEGAN TO FOLLOW the route of Odysseus in my thirty-five-foot sailing yacht I thought I would merely tell about my modern voyage. But I soon discovered that when I told my friends what I was doing and mentioned the Lotus Eaters, Polyphemus, and Circe, (and place names like Thrace, Corfu, and Djerba), I received polite stares of confusion.

Little by little I learned that while most people know about Odysseus and the Trojan Horse, and may agree with the reports that Helen was radiant, statuesque, and divine, the truth is that fewer people than you think have actually read *The Iliad* and *The Odyssey*. These are books that people plan to read or should have read or tried to read in the ninth grade, but somehow didn't. "Too long, too difficult, and all those terrible unpronounceable names." To make sense of my modern parallel journey, I realized that I would have to tell bits of the ancient story here and there.

Odysseus appears to have made nineteen stops during his ten-year trip around the Mediterranean. Our direct route in following the ancient Greek added up to 2,650 miles, but in chasing after clues, retracing routes, wintering, going back and forth, and so on we logged 6,500 miles. By the time we sailed back to Chesapeake Bay in the U.S. from where we had started, we logged 18,132 miles. It was a lot of sailing, but except for a few days, all the miles were pleasant.

I hope this book will encourage you to read the wonderful verse translations by Robert Fagles, Alexander Pope, and others, and sing along with Homer's timeless, enduring, golden lines. I've tried hard to be accurate and precise, but *The Odyssey* is not accurate and precise. It's a story about people first and places second. Some may object to the fine points of my route, but nitpicking is unimportant. Read and enjoy Homer for pleasure, not from a sense of obligation or duty.

A word about Greek place names: it seems that the independent Greeks—who seldom agree about anything—spell the names of cities, villages, bays, rivers, etc., in many ways. For example, the Ionian island of Kefallinía is spelled Kephallinia, Kephalinia, Cephallinia, Cefallinia, or Cefhallinia (with or without the accent on the final i). Take your pick. In general I have used the spellings on British Admiralty sailing charts (whose compilers also fought this battle) except in the cases where a name has become so well-known that it seems foolish to use an alternate. Hence Ithaca instead of Itháki, Thiaki, Ithaki, or Ithakee. Cape Malea instead of Akra Maléas, and so forth.

While checking a few spellings I made the mistake of asking the advice of one Greek while another Greek listened in. In less than thirty seconds they were arguing at the tops of their voices.

"You can spell it that way, but it's wrong."

"But that's how my mother spelled it. Are you impugning the teachings of my mother?"

"No, but she was misinformed."

"So my mother's a liar?"

"Of course not. It's just that˙. . ."

"Let's step outside. . . ."

My thanks to Jim Calvert, Michael Comparone, Fotiní Couvaras, Jim Gieske, Tom Mann, Saranatis Symeonoglou, and Gerry Warwick who helped. And to ever-faithful Margaret.

WE FOLLOWED
ODYSSEUS

View northwest from Troy toward the Dardanelles, the great seaway between the Aegean and the Black Sea. The two women are standing up on the ruins of Troy, which in the ancient world was rebuilt nine times, the new always constructed on the ruins of the old.

A VISIT
TO TROY

ARGARET AND I ARE SITTING in the doubtful shade of a pathetic olive tree at a sun-baked ancient ruin called *Hisarlik* in the northwestern corner of Turkey. We're up about 20 meters above the surrounding countryside and looking over the fertile flood plain of the Menderes river. Enormous fields of ripe cotton lie beneath us, and in the distance we can see the bobbing head scarves of women pickers as they deftly pluck the white tufts and drop them into wicker baskets. In other fields women pick big red tomatoes and stack them in wooden boxes. Farther away, about four kilometers to the northwest, we can just make out the Dardanelles—the waterway coming from the Sea of Marmara—where it meets the Aegean.

While we unwrap our sandwiches and eat lunch we look out at the wide blue of the strait and the white spears of the distant lighthouses. I count four large ships—two bound eastward toward the Black Sea, and two low oil tankers heading westward.

Hisarlik—which means little fortress—the mound of partially excavated ruins we're sitting on—is the site of ancient Troy. The Troy of Homer, the famous battleground where ordinary mortals, kings, and gods supposedly fought one another during the Trojan War of 1200 B.C., almost thirty-two centuries ago. The Troy beneath us is the Troy of *The Iliad*. The Troy of *The Odyssey*. The Troy that was forgotten and thought to be in Homer's imagination until it was dug into by Heinrich Schliemann in

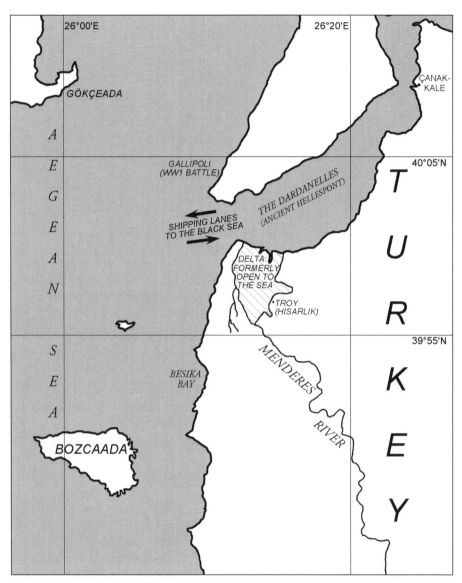

THE DARDANELLES

1873 when he startled the world with the announcement that he had discovered King Priam's golden treasure from the ancient world. In the one hundred and twenty-five years since Schliemann, five generations of archeologists have probed and analyzed the ruins. [1]

The first Troy was built in the dim mists of history and became prominent because it controlled the trade on the vital northeast waterway between the Mediterranean and the Black Sea. The fort was a large irregular rectangle surrounded by unclimbable stone walls and ringed by thriving settlements (women spinning and weaving, craft shops, pottery kilns), rich farmland (fruit trees, vegetables, grain), and a boating community (fish, shellfish, patrol vessels).

By the middle of the thirteenth century B.C., the time of our story, archeologists tell us that Troy had risen and fallen seven times because of earthquakes, fires, and wars. But after each setback the great fort rose to prominence again, perhaps mightier than ever. Now the Trojans traded copper, tin, iron, fine woods, pottery, wine, dyes, hides, spices, perfumes, jewelry, wheat, and horses. In addition Troy squeezed its neighbors and made them pay. Silver, for example, was mined nearby and a share of the bright metal went to the city. (The polite term was tribute, but muscle was everything in those days.) It was an era of hit-and-run raiding parties, the big fist, the long spear, the strong over the weak. Through it all, Troy stood firm and impregnable behind thick walls, massive gates, tough defenders, and a big treasury.

But commerce is never static. Even though the Hittites dominated much of Asia, the Mycenaeans were establishing towns and competing trade centers in what is now Turkey. True, the Mycenaeans were friends of the Trojans, but Troy was a special problem, an obstacle, and the Mycenaeans began to cast covetous eyes at the fort. The Hittite empire was falling apart, and a natural disaster—an earthquake—rattled the walls of Troy. Maybe Troy was no longer invincible. Perhaps 1200 B.C. was the time to strike. The motives were clear, and it took only the incident of Paris and Helen to set off the conflict for control of the waterway.

"But how?" you might ask if you looked around today, "could Troy control the Dardanelles from a distance of four kilometers from the sea?" The answer is that in the thirteenth century B.C., the waters of the Dardanelles lapped close to the settlement; Troy had marsh and water on two sides. Today the accumulated river silt of thirty-two centuries has built up a delta that extends northwest for four kilometers, and isolates Troy from the sea.

In the ancient world the only dry land approaches were from the east or south. With a few armed patrol vessels the Trojans easily watched the straits and Besika bay on the Aegean side. In addition the weather was on the tax collector's side. Because of persistent northeasterly headwinds, the leg up the Dardanelles was (is) slow and tedious. Whether they wanted to or not, transiting boats usually had to stop somewhere in the Troy area and wait for a favorable slant of wind. This could take a day or it could take weeks. No doubt the area was a meeting place of captains and crews, a stop where information and gossip and a few cups of wine were exchanged while the supercargoes paid their tariffs, which couldn't have been too high or the charges would have killed the trade. Sometimes impatient shippers unloaded their goods and continued overland with pack animals.

At the time of the Trojan War the fighting ships were slim, open, canoe-type vessels, somewhat on the order of college racing shells, only larger and heavier-built. Homer speaks of two sizes: the twenty-oared and the fifty-oared. The smaller was about fifty-five feet long and ten feet wide; the larger was one hundred feet in length and proportionally beamier. In those days the helmsmen steered with oars because the rudder had yet to be invented.[2]

In calms or light headwinds the crews moved the fighting ships by pulling on long oars. With a fair breeze the men stowed the oars and hoisted a squaresail for downwind sailing or perhaps across the wind. The rigs were low and primitive, however, and quite useless to windward. At night the sailors generally ran their light-weight ships up on a convenient beach. During the winter the vessels were laid up ashore.

The cargo ships were beamier, partially decked, heavier-built, and harder to move. Instead of the adjectives "sleek and stream-lined," the operative words were "bulky and ponderous." The trips of these merchant vessels must have been incredibly slow when faced with headwinds because their windward horsepower was limited to the rowing effort of the crew, which was good for only a few miles. The sailors had to play daily wind shifts and deal with seasonal wind changes. The real game was to stop and wait for fair winds.

In addition the cargo ships were too big and heavy to be run up on beaches at night. Sheltered harbors and suitable anchoring techniques became necessary. This introduced a whole set of new problems. There were no charts, so a captain had to memorize a coastline and its anchorages. Yet the anchors of the time were small and flimsy. A captain carried a dozen spares when he set out on a long trip. The ropes that he used for his anchor cables were crude, of uncertain strength, and the natural fibers often broke. There must have been times when everything seemed to conspire against him. The ancient mariner must have been a very patient fellow.

Clay jug of the 7th century B.C. from the Aegean island of Skíros. Note the wonderful thin black horses with long necks and tails.

The magnetic compass, the ship's log, and the nautical chart were far in the future, and offshore navigation as we practice it today was only a dream in the night. Men rowed or sailed from one familiar point of land to another. During a risky overwater passage they steered by the sun or certain stars. To appease the gods and strengthen their resolve against the unknown—particularly when going out of sight of land—the early voyagers ritually sacrificed cattle or sheep before starting. The sailors then built a big fire, cooked the meat, and stuffed themselves (usually with a few cups of sweet wine, no doubt filched from the cargo) to fortify their spirits and bodies for the upcoming, hazardous passage.

I WAS THRILLED TO VISIT TROY. It was wonderful to see the famous place where the Trojan War was fought so long ago. However Homer's epic suggests that Troy was an enormous city with tens of thousands of cheering residents. Most visitors soon exclaim: "Is this all there is? Where's the rest of it?"

I had vaguely heard about "the city of Troy," but the tumbledown ruin on which Margaret and I sat measured only 150 x 200 meters. In the old days there must have been an extensive satellite settlement of towns and villages around the walled citadel, but centuries of winter rains, occasional floods, and scorching summer sun have wiped out all traces of the houses, shops, roadways, and market places. The blacksmith's forge is long gone, and the pottery kilns blew to dust a thousand years ago. The foundation stones were dragged away for building elsewhere or broken up for road paving. Clumps of brush and trees have grown up, and today much of the earth has been plowed and planted with cotton and tomatoes. What we see of Troy these days is merely the central remnant—the comma from a paragraph—a very small place.

As I walked around the ancient fortress I thought of the pages of *The Iliad* in which Homer talked about the vastness of Troy, the gigantic battles, and the superhuman individual combat. I began to realize that Homer was a poet, a creative artist, a storyteller. Exaggeration and hyperbole were two of his writing tools. He stretched and embroidered many things. His writing sparkles with golden words, but his facts are often puffed up and marvelous:

"A thousand fires were burning in the plain, and round each there sat fifty men in the gleam of the blazing fire." Well maybe, but the reader had better drop a zero from the numbers.

"He had three thousand horses herded in the fens. All mares, proud with their soft, young foals." Three thousand? Really?

The Trojan War was said to last ten years. Two is probably closer to the truth. Can you imagine the problems of trying to make a rag-tag mob of itinerant sea raiders cooperate and fight side by side during the difficult siege of a fortress? For ten years? With a flawed command structure? Particularly with a group of hot-headed Greek irregulars who often squabbled among themselves and were as independent as stones rolling down a mountainside. We won't even discuss the horrendous problems of sanitation and disease.

Homer's mountains are always the highest. The women are radiant and beguiling. The men are tall, wide-shouldered, and super-strong. Everyone is a hero, the best, the brightest. The fortress is vast and impregnable. Each bronze spear is the sharpest ever known. Every drug is magical. And so on and on.

Ancient Greece has made so many contributions to western culture, science, and politics that we think that it was the same size as modern Greece. The truth is that populations were much smaller in the old days. Athens, the biggest city in Greece during the time of Homer, had a population of 300,000 including slaves and foreigners. Athens today has about three and a half million people, almost twelve times more. [3]

I began to understand that the places Margaret and I sought would have to be viewed through those trick circus eyeglasses that make the big appear small and the wide narrow. Those distorting mirrors at a fun house that turn skinny boys into fat men and short women into tall giants. I don't want to be a party-pooper or a kill-joy, but I hope to deal with Homer on real-life terms. Is this possible? And who am I to try to de-mystify the man? I have no desire to strip away the illusions of mystery and wonder, but simply to follow the route of Odysseus.* Yet to understand Odysseus I will have to find out about Homer by trying to fathom his strengths and weaknesses. I will have to unravel the tricks of his craft.

---

*Odysseus is often called Ulysses, the Roman version of our subject's name. Since we are dealing with earlier Grecian times we will stick to the name given by Homer.

Yacht Whisper *sailing nicely in light airs.*

THE BEGINNING

ON JUNE 20, 1995 we sailed from Chesapeake Bay in the U.S. to far-off Turkey in the eastern Mediterranean in our thirty-five-foot sloop *Whisper*. The voyage via the Azores and Gibraltar took us fifty days, and we logged 5,123 miles. As on earlier trips Margaret and I sailed by ourselves, and we took turns standing three- or four-hour watches.

It was mostly an easy, peaceful trip. According to the Atlantic pilot charts we should have had moderate southwesterlies, but we experienced winds from every direction. It breezed up a couple of times and forced us down to three reefs in the mainsail, but the light weather soon returned. Once far out in the Atlantic we were surrounded by thousands of big yellowfin tuna that swam alongside us for three days. When we reached the Strait of Gibraltar we ran into a foggy, forty-five-knot headwind that blew us back to Cadiz, Spain, where we waited a few days until the strong easterly eased off.

Margaret, my dear wife, was keen to make this trip. She's the greatest of travelers and is always ready to sail to such places as the Strait of Magellan, the Aleutian Islands, or northern Australia. As long as we're going somewhere, she never complains, makes sensible suggestions, and has rescued me from a thousand quicksands into which I've stepped because of my impetuous and foolhardy nature. She likes to experiment with cooking. Her spice rack's a mess, but her sauces are wonderful. She dresses well, but she's liable to repair a dropped hem with a stapling machine rather than with a needle and thread. She can't whistle, but she's good at rowing a dinghy. She likes to knit and is a nut on crossword puzzles. She has such a generous nature that she'd cheerfully give her last cent to a beggar or a child. In a crisis (sailing is full of crises) she's as steady as a granite cliff. I forgive her for being slightly disorganized and for losing things.

OUR MAGIC CARPET for the trip was *Whisper*, a beamy masthead sailing sloop designed by the British naval architects Holman & Pye. The vessel was exquisitely built by Henri Wauquiez in France in 1984. She belongs to the Pretorien class and is #143 of the series. Her hull and deck are fiberglass, and she has an external lead keel.

Her dimensions:

Overall length	10.67 meters	35' 4½"
Waterline length	8.82 meters	28' 11½"
Draft	1.88 meters	6' 2"+
Beam	3.63 meters	11' 11"
Mast height above WL	16.58 meters	54' 5" (a tall rig)
Displacement	6.43 m. tons	14,184 pounds
Keel weight	2.94 m. tons	6,490 pounds
Sail area: main + fore ▲	59.5 sq. meters	640½ sq. feet

We had the usual gear on board for long distance sailing: a Monitor wind vane steering gear, an autopilot, a hand-operated anchor windlass, five anchors and warps, and sixty meters of 3/8" chain. We took along two spinnaker poles, an eight-foot hard rowing dinghy plus a small inflatable, a big awning, lots of extra line, and masses of tools and spare parts. We started out with three new sails: a mainsail, a 110 percent full hoist jib, and a 130 percent genoa. We loaded on a spare mainsail, a working jib, a storm jib, and a spinnaker. We carried 250 liters of fresh water (66 U.S. gallons) and 95 liters (25 gallons) of diesel fuel. The engine was a three-cylinder Volvo-Penta 2003 of 23 horsepower with a two-bladed 17" dia. x 14" pitch Martec folding propeller. We cooked on a two-burner kerosene stove and carried a large selection of food on board.

I think Odysseus would have liked our vessel.

BOTH ON THIS VOYAGE and on an earlier trip we found that the winds in the Mediterranean were generally less than in the Atlantic. Except for sitting out a few calms, however, we managed to keep going under sail. We had a fresh following wind along the coast of Tunisia, and at Cape Bon we raced along in smooth water with a double-reefed mainsail. In light running winds we set our red, yellow, and black spinnaker. It made a lot of swishing noises, but kept us going hour after hour.

We enjoyed the peace and quiet of the long ocean voyage, and the weeks of solitude put us in the mood to consider our main objective: *to retrace the voyages of Odysseus.* We planned to sail everywhere the ancient Greek adventurer traveled—or supposedly traveled—to find out whether Homer's great epic poem made any sense to us. Margaret and I hoped to answer a multiple-choice question.

1. Is the story fantasy?
2. Is the story based on a light framework of fact?
3. Or is the story true with bits of a writer's make-believe thrown in?

Why in God's name would anyone want to go to the trouble of retracing the voyages of a prickly Greek who may not have even existed? To hunt up obscure places with unpronounceable names in out-of-the-way islands and coastlines? To fight through confusing and conflicting histories and accounts written by authors who seldom agree about anything? To try to explain mysterious kingdoms, confusing battles, one-eyed monsters, and sirens who lured sailors with a wink and a shapely leg? All tied to events that happened thousands of years ago.

Why waste time on a doubtful voyage written (or dictated or imagined) by a supposed blind poet who may never have lived? Whose verses may have been written by a committee. Edited by critics. Changed by scribes. Modified by copyists. No one knows the details, and it's doubtful that hard evidence will surface from tombs and ruins because archeologists have been picking over the dusty soil of Italy, Greece, Turkey, and Egypt for centuries. The poems are obscure; the poet a mystery. The whole thing is a sort of double negative, a mark in the dark, rumor, conjecture, guesswork, make-believe.

Yet—ah, there's the pregnant word!—yet sailors and writers have been fascinated by Homer for almost three thousand years. Every year or two a Greek scholar or a French archeologist adds a book to the pile. Why? Because the tales are just true enough to be possible. Just mythical enough to be on the tippy border between fantasy and maybe-land. In 1996, Viking published a stunning edition of a new translation of *The Odyssey* by Princeton professor Robert Fagles, and by September 1998 it had sold 80,000 copies in hardback and 100,000 in paper. The royalties have made the author a wealthy man.

Margaret and I knew that at one time the poem was thought to be a romantic daydream. A strange relic of the ancient world. Yet the story of the Trojan War (*The Iliad*, the first war book), and the travels of a rascal named Odysseus (*The Odyssey*, about a man's flight home from war) have been read and admired for twenty-eight centuries. The two books form the bedrock of culture of the western world. They are the originals for every tale of human conflict, and as historian Barbara Tuchman has pointed out, have belonged to all the people all this time—even before literacy began.[4]

For centuries, readers enjoyed the stories but thought them entirely imaginary. However archeological discoveries at Troy and Mycenae since the 1870s, and recent work at the Palace of Nestor at Pylos and other ancient Greek sites suggest that much of Homer's writing was in fact based on a real world. Readers now know that the Greece of long ago was a complex, highly organized, culture-rich society.

The walls of the great palace of King Nestor at Pylos in the western Pelopónnisos, for example, were graced with bright frescoes of blue and red and green, often with paintings of mythical animals and plants and flowers. The high ceilings, supported with large round columns, were patterned with intricate decorations. Shimmering embroideries, often dyed a deep blue, hung at eye level, and the polished mosaic floors glowed with a dull brightness. The leaders were well-groomed and nicely dressed and sat on fine furniture or on soft rugs of fleece. Their drinking vessels were often of gold decorated with silver or blue enamel, and they ate from elegant pottery of a dozen varieties.

The whole place sounds rather upbeat and elegant. With information like this, ancient Greece and the writings of Homer don't seem so remote and far away.[5]

Even in an age of computers and travel by jet aircraft, children know about Troy and the Trojan horse. *"The Odyssey"* is on every schoolteacher's list. When I asked my neighbor's twelve-year-old Teresa about Odysseus, she replied:

"Homer [she confused Odysseus with Homer] was a Greek who sailed and rowed around a bunch of islands out there somewhere and had adventures with some far-out people. He didn't make it back home until he was an old man. His wife Penelope was still waiting, but his house was full of men who were trying to make out with her. He had to kill them all so he could have a little peace and quiet. It's a sort of Greek western without the horses, but with good guys and bad guys." Teresa then gave Homer the ultimate accolade of today's young people: "He was cool," she said. "Real cool."

Homer's stories operate on a high and complex level, and almost every human emotion—joy, sorrow, greed, envy, hate, jealousy, love—you name it—is displayed along with an intriguing amount of sex. There are skillful time changes, sparkling dialogue, and plenty of fresh characters. You know right away that the author was a storyteller of great skill.[6]

In truth, however, little is known about Homer. His birthplace was along the western coast of what today is Turkey or on one of the nearby offshore islands in the eastern Aegean. The exact place is in doubt (Smyrna, Chios, Kyme, perhaps Colophon). No one knows when he was born (the best estimate is 800 B.C.), how he was educated, or when he died. Homer is usually said to have been blind, an oral reciter of tales, a poor wandering minstrel. Tradition says that he simply embellished existing oral traditions and may have dictated his tales to scribes around 750 B.C.—about the time that writing was becoming known in the region. Later Greek and Roman commentators claim that Homer left nothing in writing; that the stories were put together by others from legends of different places. Others believe that Homer's stories were transmitted orally from father to son until the tales were written down in Athens several hundred years later.

We have reports of an authoritative Athenian text in the sec-

A modern (1990) fifty-drachma coin with an artist's conception of Homer. No one, of course, has the faintest idea what Homer looked like, but he is generally represented as a middle-aged fellow with long hair, a headband, and a look of contemplative wisdom. In Greek, his name is spelled ΟΜΕΡΟΣ, *which in English letters is OMEROS.*

ond half of the sixth century B.C. Papyrus copies of it have come down to us, but even some of these copies vary significantly.[7] Certainly changes crept in as the stories were copied and re-copied by hand. Experts attempted to deal with these variations and to establish "true" copies, but like relics of "the true cross," the problem is which are genuine and which are simply scraps of junk wood?

I like the image of Homer reciting to an audience of excited listeners in one of those shell-shaped stone Greek theaters that were the feature of every ancient Greek town. Experts tell me that these Greek theaters were unknown in Homer's time, but there must have been some meeting place where he performed.

We don't know whether Homer composed his verses as he went along or delivered long set pieces. It's likely that he memorized and used certain formal introductions and endings and composed the central parts as he spoke, tailoring the material to his audience.

In the real world, a narrator or entertainer or professor talks for only an hour or at the most two because anything longer either loses the audience or puts everyone to sleep. Also an hour or two is about the limit of a performing artist's energy. To have recited the entire *Iliad* would have taken twenty hours, so either the narrator spoke on succeeding days or nights (the first soap opera?) or the stories were cut and shortened. This suggests editing and abridgment into convenient chunks of verse. No wonder there's disagreement about the text![8]

Over the centuries a vast audience of ordinary people have enjoyed Homer's two epic poems. Readers have marveled at the struggles between the Greeks and the Trojans, the gods vs. the mortals, the Trojan horse, and Odysseus's long voyage home. Meanwhile scholars have nit-picked and disputed every point (authorship, historical accuracy, locations, purity of translation, and so on). The books, opinions, and research on Homer and his works would fill a small library and require a reader to know three or four languages. Before I left the U.S., I visited the Library of Congress in Washington and found 196 primary books on the subject. Plus several thousand secondary sources. All this stuff was a bit daunting.

Aboard our little yacht *Whisper* we had a mere thirty-four books about Homer and his work. Fortunately we had several compensating advantages. Instead of being in an ivory tower in London, Berlin, or Paris we were on the spot and busy looking at the real world of Odysseus. Though we didn't have his large group of men, we knew that *Whisper's* sailing ability was vastly superior to the ancient Greek vessels and that we could make do with only two people. We didn't have expert rowers, but we could sail to windward, something impossible for Odysseus's squaresail. We had excellent charts, good navigational systems, and better anchors. Unlike most writers I live on the sea and have a background of sailing in many waters. Margaret and I planned to look carefully at each site or supposed site. Our heads weren't filled with the opinions of others. We were in an ideal situation to evaluate the entire poem.

What would we find in our search for Odysseus?

WE GLIDED INTO the Turkish port of Kuşadasi in mid-September after a sixteen-day non-stop sail from Gibraltar. Kuşadasi was our first Turkish port, and we were amazed to see five giant cruise ships in the harbor and hundreds of varnished Turkish charter motor yachts (gulets, pronounced goo-LETS) lined up along the waterfront. Thousands of mostly German tourists were strolling up and down eating ice cream cones and buying brass paperweights and fake Greek pottery made of plastic. The local economy was utterly dependent on tourism, and the carpet sellers, taxi drivers, and restaurants touts were in a frenzy. What, I wondered, would Homer have thought of this scene? Were there tourists in Homer's day? How did they make it without airlines, travel agents, and Visa cards?

I reminded myself that electric lights, refrigeration, diesel engines, trains, automobiles, radios, and computers didn't exist in 750 B.C. Gunpowder was unknown. Photography hadn't been invented. Every bit of cloth was woven by hand. Writing as we practice it was only being introduced; printing, advertising, and books were still to come. The ancient Greeks had no idea of modern medical care. How did they get through life without cellular phones, hi-fi sets, television, and CNN? (Answer: Very well, thank you. We used our leisure to develop our arts, thoughts, and government.) Lest we glorify the ancient Greeks too much, however, don't forget that the privileged class exploited slaves to the maximum and sometimes treated unfortunates or enemies with appalling cruelty. There was no concept of human rights at all; the man with the fist ruled everything in sight. Women, meek and in the shadows, existed for the pleasure of men, to raise children, and to weave and cook.

MARGARET AND I HURRIED BACK to *Whisper* and fled from the hordes of tourists in Kuşadasi. We sailed north-northwest along the Aegean coast of Turkey toward Troy, our initial target. Much of the coastline is wild and mountainous and gorgeous; fortunately it's all well charted. We reminded ourselves that sailing along an intricate coast is quite different from voyaging on the ocean where you keep going twenty-four hours a day and try to cover as much distance as possible. Our concern now was not mileage, but to keep from hitting the rocks, so we moved in little jumps that we could make during daylight hours. We anchored every night and saw few tourists. Life aboard *Whisper* was peaceful and quiet.

We worked north of the Greek islands of Khios and Lesvos and crept past the towering headlands and barren mountains along the Turkish mainland. We stopped at Kirkdilum, Çesme, Yenifoca,

Alibey, and Bozcaada (ancient Tenedos).* The next day we sailed another twelve miles north-northeast and reached the Dardanelles, the great strait that runs northeast to the Black Sea. Now we were in major shipping lanes. Huge container ships and oil tankers rumbled past us at twenty knots, going like sleds on ice. We aimed for Çanakkale, thirteen miles farther upstream and the closest port to Troy. We had come 233 miles from Kuşadasi.

In six days of sailing (sixty hours) we averaged thirty-nine miles made good per day. Not very good for a modern yacht, but I use the excuse of light winds, a lot of tacking, and calms. Odysseus's fighting ships could probably have done better than our paltry 3.9 knot average. Were we superior to the ancient Greeks? Absolutely not! So far they were the clear winners.

Çanakkale (cha-KNOCK-a-lee) is fifteen miles up the Dardanelles on the south side of the strait, a bustling city of 57,000 involved in light manufacturing and fruit and vegetable distribution. Tourists come to visit Troy and the battlefields of Gallipoli. We found the harbor a frantic place that was chock-a-block with fishing boats of all sizes and bustling car ferries that rushed back and forth across the strait. The port had a fleet of agent boats—speedy launches that flew enormous Turkish flags and hurried out to merchant ships steaming through the Dardanelles. The agent boats took out specialist mechanics, dealt with paperwork, delivered duty-free whiskey to cruise liners, changed crew members, delivered spare parts, and so forth.

Because of the prevailing northeast winds I had been warned to tie to a windward dock in Çanakkale. The local boats had all the good places, however, and we were directed to a leeward dock. I dropped a stern anchor and tied *Whisper's* bow next to a heavy wooden Turkish yacht named *Pavurya*. She was fourteen meters long with a big engine and a short rig on a solid wooden mast. As we pulled alongside, her owner and his wife came on deck, and we met Ali Ayhan and his wife Nilay. Ali was a big, tough-looking, outgoing Turk with a dazzling smile who spoke some English. Nilay, also tall, with wonderfully attractive large dark eyes, appeared behind Ali, a bit shy because she spoke no English.

---

*See endpaper map.

Ali Ayhan with his daughter Deniz sitting in Whisper's *cabin.*

Ali warned me about the northeast wind and the dock behind us. "The anchor must be good," he said. "I can help you." Again I got his dazzling smile. We waved Ali and Nilay aboard for a look at *Whisper*. We learned that a few years earlier, *Pavurya* (which means crab) had been an abandoned hulk. Ali, working mostly alone, had rebuilt her into a trim yacht that he and his family had lived on for a year. Deniz, their daughter, was six and had just started school. She was playing with the daughter of Ali's assistant, Hassan, who appeared with a paintbrush. Although the weather was blustery, Ali and Hassan were sanding and painting *Pavurya's* decks and bulwarks with metallic blue paint. Ali, who was forty-nine, was a salvage diver and had worked all over the world. He was trying to start his own salvage company and like many businessmen had snappy business cards. Ali carried a cellular phone (the bronze spear of the 1990s) everywhere with him, always hoping for The Big Call.

Margaret made tea for everyone, and Nilay watched fascinated as Margaret primed the kerosene stove and moved around *Whisper's* galley. During the next few days between visits to Troy we spent a lot of time with the Ayhans. Margaret—using her dictionary—asked Nilay for a Turkish recipe. As a result we were invited aboard *Pavurya* to sample Turkish food. Nilay was a whiz in her galley. She would cook special local delicacies: eggplant halves with onions, meat, and peppers, or zucchini stuffed with savory rice and tomatoes. Then she would rap on *Whisper's* hull, and hand across a steaming plateful.

As predicted, on the second night the northeast wind freshened to thirty knots. Ali helped me with a second anchor, which we laid out on a very long line. Then—because the depth was only three meters—we sank the anchor line with a heavy lead weight so the propellers of the work boats wouldn't cut the nylon. The following night the harbor was cold and nasty, and it blew forty knots. (My thoughts and sympathies were with those ancient mariners who had also hung on in the strait while they waited for a wind shift.) Ali laid out a second anchor for his boat and threw me a line so that *Whisper* lay partially to it. My new Turkish friend was keen to practice English, so the next day we talked for a long time.

Ali had all sorts of salvaged gear on his boat. He didn't like to sell things, but to swap for other equipment that might be useful in the future. He was a born trader, an innovator, a practical engineer, not a business type although he was scrambling for salvage contracts. My Turkish neighbor had the practiced motions of a real seaman, but I had the distinct feeling that he was also a pirate of sorts, a bit of a rascal, a Long John Silver with a twinkle in his eye. He was smart and clever, always looking around, sizing up people and what they were doing, and wondering if he could do it better. Could there have been the faintest trace of Odysseus—that adventurer of so long ago—in this man that I met near Troy?

In 1959, workmen digging a sewer in Piraeus discovered a whole set of sensational bronze statues, including this marvelous form of Athena in military garb. Larger than life, today this breathtaking Athena towers over all the other exhibits at the Piraeus Archeological museum. Experts theorize that the statues were buried and forgotten while waiting shipment to Rome when a warehouse where they were stored burned down, probably in the Sullan sack of 86 B.C. Note how the sculptor has decorated the battle helmet and breastplate with small birds and mythical animals. His goal was not to overpower these instruments of war, but to suggest that even in conflict there can be beauty.

THE ILIAD
IN 1,952 WORDS

O K, WE'VE VISITED TROY. Now we need to find out about Odysseus. Before we talk about him let's have a quick look at *The Iliad*, the book that introduced him to the world.

THE YEAR WAS 1230 B.C. when Odysseus, the young king of Ithaca, a small island kingdom off the northwest coast of Greece, made a proposition to Tyndareus, the king of mainland Sparta.

Tyndareus was the foster-father of Helen, a skinny teenager who had suddenly become a beautiful young woman. A dozen young men with prestigious credentials desperately wanted to marry her, particularly since her father was the great Zeus and her mother was Leda, queen of Sparta. Helen's suitors tried to influence Tyndareus by offering him expensive presents, each more lavish than the last.

Tyndareus was at his wit's end. If he accepted the presents he'd be obligated to the donors. If he turned the men away, Helen would be wretched and unhappy and blame him. If the men fought over Helen, the palace would become a bloody battlefield. Tyndareus despaired. He didn't know what to do. At that moment Odysseus, who was one of the young men who wanted to marry Helen, but who realized that his chances were slim because he represented only a small kingdom, spoke privately to Tyndareus:

"Sire, I see a way out of your troubles."

"What's that?" asked Tyndareus.

"If I can show you how to avoid bloodshed and find an easy solution, will you put in a good word for me with your brother Icarius? I want to marry your niece Penelope."

"Little Penelope? Really? Well . . . yes, I suppose so," said Tyndareus who was intrigued. "What's your idea?"

"Here's the plan," said Odysseus. "Collect all the suitors together. Tell them you're about to make the final selection. Tell them there can be only one winner. Tell them that someone in the group may feel insulted and seek revenge. Tell them they must all take a solemn oath to accept your decision, and additionally, the group must promise to bind together to punish anyone who interferes with your decision and takes Helen by force. Explain to the suitors that they must agree in order to have a chance for Helen."

"Brilliant!" replied Tyndareus, clapping his hands together. He quickly called a meeting of the suitors and outlined the arrangement. All the suitors—including Odysseus—took the oath.

Shortly afterwards, Tyndareus made his big announcement: "I've picked Menelaus, the young brother of King Agamemnon, the ruler of Mycenae and Argos and the overlord of the region, to marry Helen," he said. "In time the royal couple will assume the throne of Sparta."

Menelaus and Helen were married; together they ruled Sparta. All went well, and after a time they had a daughter named Hermione. During the tenth year of his reign, Menelaus traveled to Troy on business and met Paris, a local prince. They became friends, and Menelaus invited Paris to visit him. Paris accepted and traveled to Sparta where he stayed in the palace and met Helen.

Paris was no ordinary prince. He was handsome and clever, but devious and scheming; resourceful, but with a hollow heart. Aphrodite, the goddess of Love, had already promised him Helen. So when he made eyes at her she reciprocated. King Menelaus received news from Crete that his father had died. He set off at once for the funeral. While he was gone, Paris and Helen ran off together.

In the eyes of the Greeks it was a terrible sin for a guest to take advantage of his host. To abscond with his host's wife was even worse—particularly when the host was king and the hostess was queen. But Helen was so entranced with Paris that she even left her nine-year-old daughter behind. In a final outrage she took some of the palace treasures; Paris helped himself to gold and silver from Sparta's temple of Apollo.

The two lovers sailed to Cyprus where Paris put together a raiding party that sacked the city of Sidon and collected more gold and silver. Paris then took Helen to Troy. Her beauty awed King Priam and

Head of a woman in plaster from the 13th century B.C., the era of the Trojan War. Perhaps Helen decorated her face in the same manner with eye shadow and these small red circles surrounded with red dots.

the Trojans, and they told her she could stay forever. There were a few critics, but Paris silenced them with gifts of gold.

When King Menelaus discovered that his wife had eloped with Paris, and his palace and temple had been robbed he was outraged. He sent word to his brother, Agamemnon, and instructed him to summon armed help from each of the suitors. Agamemnon, trying to avoid war, told Menelaus to be patient. Meanwhile he sent envoys to Troy. King Priam made the usual excuses: "If Helen left with my son, Paris, and they took gold from the palace and the temple, she must have been part of the scheme. In any case, Paris isn't here."

Agamemnon promptly called up the men who had taken the oath to help Menelaus. "We'll attack Troy," he said. "The place is loaded with treasure, and once it falls we can divide the loot. Besides, we pay too much in tribute for goods from the Black Sea. As soon as we overrun Troy, the way through the Hellespont will be open and clear!"

The greatest find of the German archeologist Heinrich Schliemann was this gold death mask that he discovered in the ancient Greek city of Mycenae in 1876. Schliemann proclaimed that he had found the death mask of Agamemnon and sent his famous telegram to the King of Greece "congratulating him on the discovery of his ancestors." The gold mask was eventually found to belong to an earlier period, but is still often called "the death mask of Agamemnon" after its discoverer. This work in gold leaf is one of the principal exhibits in the National Archeological Museum in Athens. It takes a hard-hearted viewer not to feel a thrill when you first see this golden treasure.

Agamemnon collected a fleet of fighting ships from all over Greece. A thousand ships, each filled with fighting men, met at Aulis across from the island of Euboea. When the fleet was ready, Agamemnon sacrificed a hundred bulls to Zeus and Apollo to ensure the gods' blessing, but when the fleet left for Troy a storm lashed out from the northeast. Thirty percent of the fleet was lost. Seven hundred warships staggered back to Aulis.

Agamemnon learned that the gods were angry and was told to sacrifice his daughter Iphigeneia. He didn't want to do it and tried every ruse he could to save his child. However she eventually arrived at Aulis and volunteered to die for Greece. She knelt at the chopping block ready for the sacrifice. Suddenly thunder crashed and Iphigeneia disappeared, plucked from death by the goddess Artemis who whisked her away to safety. Meanwhile the ill wind from the northeast eased off. The Greek fleet headed for the Hellespont.

The men in the invading force reached Troy and forced their way ashore. They beached their ships, set up a camp, and tried to overrun the fortress. But the walls were too high, too thick, the gates too formidable, the defenses too tough, the enemy too determined. Fighting continued on the plain between the beached ships and the walled fortress. First one side would win a little; then the other. The invaders should have set up a proper siege around Troy, but they lacked the manpower and the discipline. The Trojans should have thrown the Greeks into the sea, but their fighting force was too small. The war became prolonged, frustrating, and indecisive; hand-to-hand battles raged, and the plain of Troy was splotched with blood. Much of the combat seemed to be between royalty or titled soldiers, some of whom had waiting chariots and drivers to whisk them to safety or an aid station. The fighting was complicated by the involvement of the gods who watched from their perch on Mt. Olympus and encouraged first one side, then the other.

The invaders were handicapped by the refusal of their best warrior, Achilles, to fight. After an argument with Agamemnon over a slave girl, Achilles retired to his tent where he spent most of the war sulking and feeling sorry for himself. Meanwhile Hector, one of the Trojan princes—it was now the tenth year of the war—was busy killing invaders and advancing toward the Greek fleet beached along the shore. Finally, at the last minute, when the Greeks were under heavy pressure and their ships were threatened with fire, Achilles made up with Agamemnon, put on new armor, and killed Hector. But even after the death of the great Trojan general, the Greeks were unable to take the fortified city.

War is always horrible. Especially when it's long and drawn out. Homer wrote about a spear that sliced through the tender neck of one of the Trojans:

> He fell with a crash, armor ringing against his ribs,
> his locks like the Graces' locks splashed with blood,
> still braided tight with gold and silver clips,
> pinched in like a wasp's waist. There he lay
> like an olive slip a farmer rears to strength
> on a lonely hilltop, drenching it down with water,
> a fine young stripling tree, and the winds stir it softly,
> rustling from every side, and it bursts with silver shoots—
> Then suddenly out of nowhere a wind in gale force comes
> storming, rips it out of its trench, stretches it out on the
> earth—so Panthous' stripling son lay sprawled in death . . .[9]

This strange version of the Trojan horse is on the side of a large clay pot found on the island of Míkonos in 1961, only 38 years ago. The pot dates from 675 B.C., about 525 years after the Trojan War. Since the presence of enemy soldiers was supposed to be a secret, it's unclear why this horse has handy windows cut into its sides, and whether arms are being handed in or out. Also the wheels on the horse's feet seem novel. Nevertheless we get an impression of the soldiers and their arms of the time.

Athena now told Odysseus to think up a plan to bypass the defenses of Troy. "Do something clever to get around those walls and gates," she ordered. Odysseus thought about it and called for a carpenter. During the next few days the form of an enormous hollow wooden horse began to rise above the camp. The horse was made of wooden planks with a concealed trapdoor on its left flank. There was room inside for twenty-two men to hide, including Odysseus and Menelaus.

Meanwhile the Greeks loaded their possessions on the ships, burned their camp, headed south in the Aegean, and disappeared. When the Trojans went out at dawn they found the wooden horse near the city walls. One of King Priam's councilors suggested taking the horse to Athena's temple inside the citadel. The crowd around the horse was divided and shouted back and forth.

"Smash it! Break it open with axes. Burn it! Throw it into the sea!" Others wanted to save what they thought was a sacred symbol. King Priam, uncertain what to do, decided to move the horse inside.

A Greek straggler named Sinon appeared. He told the Trojans that the wooden horse had been purposely made too large to be pushed into Troy because a prophet predicted that if the horse could be moved inside the city, the Trojans could put together an invasion of Greece and take Mycenae, Agamemnon's headquarters.

"Sinon is lying! All of this is a plant put up by Odysseus!" shouted a Trojan nobleman named Laocoön. He suggested sacrificing a bull to Poseidon, but when he was about to strike the bull with an ax, two huge snake-like monsters crawled from the sea, wrapped their bodies around Laocoön and his two sons helping him and crushed the life from all three.

The Trojans pushed the wooden horse inside the fortress and decided on a great celebration. It was then that Cassandra, one of King Priam's daughters, who had the gift of prophecy, screamed her warning: "Poor fools, you do not understand your evil fate. The horse is full of armed Greeks!"

The Trojans laughed at her, turned their backs, and began a citywide party with singing and dancing and drinking. A few hours later when the exhausted revelers were all asleep, Sinon climbed the highest wall and lit a signal torch for Agamemnon who was waiting with the fleet behind a nearby island. Then as we all know, the Greeks inside the Trojan horse opened the trapdoor and lowered themselves to the ground. They killed the sentries and unbolted the gates of the fortress. Agamemnon and his men appeared and began to kill the rest of the Trojans. Meanwhile Menelaus ran to the house where Helen lived. At first he thought of killing her, but when she looked at him he knew that she loved him. He led his wife gently back to the waiting ships.

WHO WAS ODYSSEUS?

THIRTY-TWO CENTURIES AGO, a conceited, hard-boiled king named Odysseus ruled the island of Ithaca off the northwest coast of Greece. Odysseus—like his father before him—was a good leader, stern but fair, and his edicts impressed order, stability, and a measure of prosperity on his people. Homer called him king, but in the little three-island pocket sovereignty of Ithaca, Kefallinía, and Zákinthos, which was neither rich nor poor, a better title might have been mayor, head man, or chief.

Odysseus was married to Penelope, a niece of King Tyndareus, and the couple had a son named Telemachus. They loved one another deeply and seemed set for a long and perfect life. Unfortunately before his marriage Odysseus made a fateful promise which was to cause him great suffering.

He was a man of average height, stocky, with a big chest, and strong and muscular. His beard was pointed; his hair was thick and curly; both were slightly reddish. He was a good wrestler, a speedy runner, and excelled at throwing spears. His father was Laertes, the former king. His mother was Anticlea, the daughter of Autolycus, a renowned thief and celebrated rogue, which gives us a good idea where he inherited his cunning and boldness.

When he was in his thirties, Odysseus went off to fight on foreign shores, and it was he who came up with the idea of the famous wooden horse that caused the defeat of the enemy during the Trojan War. Odysseus is also celebrated for a long and complicated voyage from Troy to Ithaca during which he survived a series of fantastic challenges whose details have become the substance of folklore and myth.

No one knows exactly where Odysseus traveled on his voyages. It appears that Homer put his most famous character into places that he heard about from far-ranging sailors. These mariners took their frail ships from the established world of the eastern Aegean (where Homer lived) to the hazy lands on the edge of the known world in the distant reaches of the western Mediterranean. Yet Homer may have known more than we think and placed his characters and actions exactly where he wanted. It's unlikely, but maybe he even traveled to some of these places. All this makes the search for the truth about Homer ever more intriguing, more difficult, probably impossible.

We're talking about the murky edge of recorded history. Homer lived about 750 B.C. The Trojan War took place around 1200 B.C., so Homer's story was based on incidents that happened about 450 years earlier—dim, unrecorded history to him. If we add 1200 B.C. to 2000 A.D., the sum is 3200, or roughly 32 centuries ago. All this is mixed up with different languages, different cultures, different people. In lands that were troubled by wars, migrations, earthquakes, and fires. No wonder the evidence is slim, vaporous, trifling. The time relationship between Homer and the Trojan War is about the same as an author of today writing about Christopher Columbus. The author faces the problem of going back 450 years when life was very different.

But back to Odysseus. When we come to his character and begin to sling adjectives at him, the list always includes words like obstinate, maddening, pig-headed, loud-mouthed, and devilish. We can easily say that he was a bully and a braggart. Yet all these words fail to categorize this wily Greek who was so intriguing, so sexually fascinating to women, always in the center of the action.

What we need is more information about the Mycenaean world (about 1580–1120 B.C.) and the wonderfully-gifted Homer who created Odysseus. All we can do is urge benefactors and governments to allocate funds so the archeologists can dig on. Meanwhile the writers speculate, and the readers scratch their heads and ask questions.

How, for example, can Odysseus be such a great leader if he lost all 616 of his men (see chapter six) on the voyage from Troy to Ithaca? Usually if a general returns without his army he's disgraced and humiliated and reaps only outrage and scorn. Not so with Odysseus. He had an answer for everything and blamed his men's problems on their stupidity, not on his ill-advised orders and faulty leadership.

Though he was bright and clever, his morals were rotten. In spite of a lot of pious talk about his men and his kingdom, Odysseus—like modern-day politicians—was interested mainly in himself. Sometimes his behavior was noble; other times despicable. At the end of his travels Odysseus hanged twelve of his palace maids for whoring with the suitors. Yet he played fast and loose with Penelope all his married life.

We first meet Odysseus in *The Iliad* at Troy. He was not the leader of the Greek forces but a middle-ranked officer who was good at backing up Agamemnon—the Greek general—whenever the war was not going well. Odysseus was full of schemes and ideas and helped pull together the Greek forces when they despaired. At one point he seized Agamemnon's scepter and took over the command himself. He screamed at the ordinary soldiers and sweet-talked the other kings into silence and compliance with the wretched command structure of the Greeks, whose officers apparently spent more time arguing with each other than fighting the Trojans. At this moment Thersites, a bitter critic, spoke up and began to hurl one insult after another at Agamemnon. He jeered at the general's appetite for pretty young women. He laughed at the leader's conceit and vanity. He scorned the chief's greed for gold and bronze.

"Agamemnon is leading us into disaster," he screamed. "Stop the bloody slaughter! We're all sick of war. It's time to go home. Let's head for the ships!"

In a twinkling Odysseus turned on Thersites. "Stop all this outrageous talk," he shouted. "Stop all these insults and indecencies. Stop all this babbling about our leader!" With that Odysseus took Agamemnon's golden scepter and began to beat Thersites across the back and shoulders. Thersites collapsed and began to cry. The men in the assembly laughed.

There was no further criticism of Agamemnon. At times Homer would have you believe that Odysseus was an Olympic champion and the paragon of all mankind. Yet at other moments he violated his word and indulged in perfidious, contemptible behavior. During the Trojan War he and another warrior were sent on a scouting mission in enemy territory and captured a soldier who knew the Trojan plans. The prisoner pleaded to be ransomed and offered a fortune in bronze and gold and well-wrought iron. Odysseus agreed to release him. Yet after the prisoner laid bare the Trojan schemes, gave details of the horsemen and chariots, and told where the enemy units lay sleeping, Odysseus and his partner killed the Trojan soldier in cold blood.

Odysseus couldn't forget an insult, and a grudge festered in his mind until he could deal with it on his own harsh terms. Before the Trojan War a man named Palamedes and others traveled to Ithaca to remind Odysseus of his pledge to fight. Odysseus—who then had a young son—didn't want to go to war. He appeared in a comic outfit trying to till a sandy beach with a horse and an ox yoked to his plow. He seemed quite mad because as he finished each furrow he sowed salt.

Palamedes saw through the king's sham to escape fighting and put Odysseus's infant son Telemachus in front of the plow. Odysseus, of course, immediately stopped the team to save his son. He began to act normally again and eventually contributed twelve ships and crews to the war. But he never forgot what Palamedes did and extracted a terrible price. During the war Odysseus planted a forged letter and gold from the Trojans in Palamedes's tent. As a result Palamedes was unjustly condemned and stoned to death. Clearly Odysseus was no man to cross.[10]

Homer's chief character may have been the first leader to discover that a politician's renown and popularity are increased by bold plans and daring schemes. No matter how outrageous the idea, no matter how far out the strategy, someone will admire him for his efforts. Enough schemes, enough talk, enough bravado, enough flag-waving, enough PR, enough spin, and a man will have built a reputation.

Odysseus might well be called a noble thug. Or an intelligent swashbuckler. My dictionary defines swashbuckler as: (1) A flamboyant swordsman or adventurer. (2) A sword-wielding ruffian or bully.

All these words describe him well.

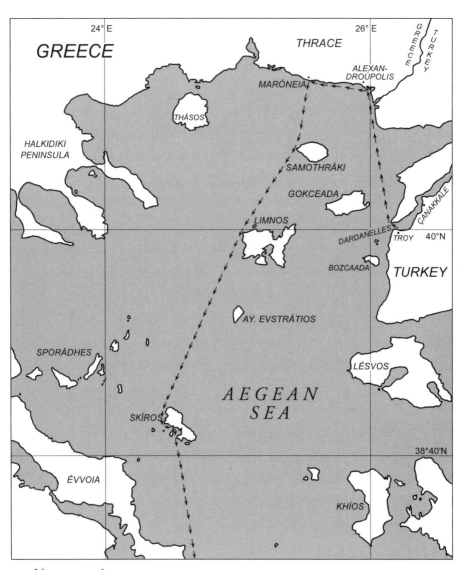

NORTHERN AEGEAN

THE 5 LAND
OF THE CICONES

O N THE DAY that Odysseus and his twelve ships left Troy for Ithaca, the wind blew from the south. Since the wind was contrary and he could not sail against it, Odysseus decided to go north instead. He would raid Ismarus, the home of the Cicones, a tribe that had sent soldiers to the defense of Troy.

The town of Ismarus lay along the mountainous seacoast of Thrace at the northeast corner of the Aegean sea; its people raised grapes, olives, grains, and livestock. The enemy fleet arrived and forced its way into the tiny seaport just below the town. The pirates swarmed ashore and soon killed most of its defenders, sacked and plundered the settlement, and divided up the women.

Odysseus—claiming respect for the gods—spared Maron, the local priest of Apollo and his wife and children. The priest responded with seven bars of wrought gold, a solid silver mixing bowl, and a dozen jars of unmixed wine from his private cache. The wine was particularly mellow, and when diluted with twenty parts of water its fumes were marvelous and irresistible. Little did Odysseus know how this wine would save his life in the days to come.

Odysseus wanted to clear out of Ismarus at once, but his men dallied, drank wine, and feasted on roasted meat from the stolen sheep and cattle. Meanwhile the Cicones rounded up powerful assistance from upcountry and attacked at dawn the next morning. Each side flung volley after volley of bronze spears at the other, but the Cicones (si-KOH-neez) were stronger. It was not a good time for Odysseus because seventy-two of his men were killed. Odysseus and the rest of his warriors jumped in their ships and fled from the wrathful defenders of Ismarus. It had been a close call for the fleet from Ithaca.

LIKE ODYSSEUS, Margaret and I left Troy and sailed for Thrace. The date was May 19th. After wintering in Turkey we were again at the mouth of the Dardanelles and sailing north in the Aegean in *Whisper.*

Big ships approached us from every direction. Giant tankers and container ships thundered past traveling east or west—in or out of the straits. Small coasting ships chugged north and south. A gaggle of fishing boats hugged the coast. To our right lay the Gallipoli peninsula and two enormous stone memorials to the terrible battle between Turkey and the Allied powers in 1915. Across the Dardanelles on our starboard quarter—hardly visible in the morning mist—loomed the Asian shore of Turkey and the dim outline of fortress Troy, a memorial to another great battle. Many people, it seemed, wanted control of these waters.

By 0940 we had worked north of the Dardanelles, left the ship traffic behind, and were sailing by ourselves. A little later a big white Turkish car ferry from the sun-baked island of Gökçeada hurried past us off to port. The fresh northeast wind from the strait began to collapse, and we idled along at two knots. Soon we were becalmed. Margaret sat on the foredeck reading *A Pair of Blue Eyes* by Thomas Hardy.

Early in the afternoon a west-northwest breeze filled in, and we were soon gliding along at five knots on smooth water. Gökçeada island fell away behind us. A little later we saw a steep mountain peak dimly floating above some low clouds off the port bow. It was the Greek island of Samothráki. As we sailed closer we marveled at the perfect cone of marble that rises 1,611 meters above the sea and is visible for miles in all directions. Why, I wondered, didn't Homer mention this prominent mountain when he told about the raiding trip that Odysseus made to the north? Every traveler along this coast was bound to see it.

By 1700 we had a good wind and were logging 6.2 knots with

the jib and one reef in the mainsail. The shores of Turkey had faded away to starboard; ahead we could see the green shores of Thrace. At 1830 we entered the harbor of Alexandroúpolis, and half an hour later tied up in the fishing port just east of a big white lighthouse. We were in a bustling commercial city of 50,000 people with banks, Greek tourists, sidewalk cafes full of garrulous old men, a bustling railroad, and outbound shipments of grain and tobacco.

We had reached Homer's land of the Cicones. What now?

The next morning I began my quest for information, which was not so easy for a foreigner to find in a place where Greek is the language. Was there a local college where I could talk to an archeologist? I found out that the local college was a medical school. When I asked about Ismarus, the taxi drivers shook their heads. "No such place," they said.

What about the newspapers? Maybe they could put me in touch with an expert or run a little story about my project. I went to two newspapers but discovered they were shopping news giveaways with mostly advertising. The little editorial work was done by several harassed women working under pressure on computers in the shadow of noisy printing presses and glowering bosses. A real sweat shop. No one spoke a word of English. I tried to contact the local stringer for an Athens newspaper, but the reporter was away.

I had a cup of coffee and went to see the harbormaster who turned out to be a great bull of a man in a trim white uniform. He was a pleasant fellow and spoke excellent English.

"You must go to the library," he said.

"Where's the library?"

"In the mayor's office on Av. Democracy." He pointed up the hill. "A couple of blocks. A modern building." He wrote the words in Greek on a slip of paper. "Show this to anyone."

The receptionist in the mayor's office—busy combing her hair—pointed to the stairs and held up four fingers. I walked up four flights to a small library and waited until the librarian, dressed in funereal black, finished talking on the telephone. "Does anyone speak English?" I asked. The librarian looked terrified and pretended to ignore me. A young woman sitting at a nearby table saved me.

"Maybe I can help," she said in English.

I introduced myself and met Stavroula Founda, a third-year college student who was studying to be a schoolteacher. I pulled out some notes, sat down next to her, and asked for information about Ismarus and the Cicones. Stavroula shook her head. Meanwhile the librarian produced a Greek history book and pointed to a few paragraphs about the Cicones, which Stavroula translated and read aloud. She didn't know all the English words, but she managed nicely by asking a student in the nearby stacks about several words. The girl from the stacks and the librarian—who now produced a map—joined our little group. Then a man pushing a baby in a stroller stopped by. He talked a lot and showed me a guidebook of Thrace written in Greek.

I was quite happy with Stavroula who was young and pretty. I secretly wished the others would go away. Nevertheless the man kept at me.

"You must come with me to a bookstore I know where you can buy a cheap copy of the Thrace guidebook in English," he said, tugging at my arm.

I reluctantly said goodbye to Stavroula and went downstairs with the man whose card said that he was Theodoros Kerkoedes, a medical librarian. ("I'm on strike," he said. "Our wages are a disgrace.") He wheeled his four-month-old infant son in the stroller out of the building and down the street with great skill. We soon arrived at the bookstore and while the owner's wife fussed over the child, Theodoros hunted up the book on Thrace. Then he and the bookstore owner, Athanasios Gialamas, had a vigorous discussion—in Greek—about my quest. Several other people in the bookstore joined in. I listened in polite ignorance.

I was told that Ismarus "is a region near Maróneia," a village on the coast twenty miles to the west. The Cicones were an early tribe in the region. There was more earnest talk—mostly in Greek, but some in English for my benefit. I was becoming aware that in Greece, opinions about *The Iliad* and *The Odyssey* are serious subjects. When I said that I was a sailor who wanted to travel to each of the places where Odysseus stopped, I saw people glance at one another and exchange nods of approval. It was nice to be surrounded by friendly intellectuals.

The medical librarian left with his child, but not until he invited me to his library ("when it's open again if those scoundrels decide to pay"). Another man appeared and began to translate the conversation (which never stopped) into English. His name was Michael Lampeas and by chance he worked at the Greek radar station on top of the 678-meter mountain that was the site of the ancient acropolis of Ismarus where the Kikkones (Greek spelling) used to live. Michael's English was quite good, and he kept up a running translation.

"I'm sorry," he said, "but you can't visit the radar station because it's a military area. We have to watch out for Turkish aircraft. There's nothing up there anyway but a few old stones and beat-up modern buildings."

Athanasios, the owner of the bookstore, handed me a book in English titled *The Wine Dark Sea* by Henriette Mertz. I read the synopsis, which suggested that Odysseus had traveled to Gibraltar, Madeira, across the Atlantic to Haiti and Cuba, north to the Bay of Fundy . . .

"What do you think?" said Athanasios.

"Preposterous," I replied, shaking my head. "The boats of that era were small and frail, largely undecked, and suitable only for fair weather sailing. During stormy seasons they were always stored on shore. Besides, how would Odysseus have traveled across the Atlantic without a compass? And back again? How could his little ships have carried enough food and water for his big crews? What about scurvy? Believe me the idea is ridiculous. It took thousands of years of ship development and improvement in sailing skills before Columbus and Magellan tried their voyages. Look at the problems they had crossing the big oceans!"

"Of course it's controversial," said Athanasios, "but we must investigate every possibility." Another man spoke about the cave of Polyphemus that was said to be nearby. But these caves are everywhere. In America, Brazil, Italy, Sicily . . .

Athanasios asked me to come back later that night. He would bring other publications. I heard about a new theory of Troy that was being worked on by a team of Greek researchers. "The real place is more to the east. Hisarlik—Troy—was only an outpost; that's why it's so small."

All this talk—was it hot air?—seemed remarkable in this tiny book-store in remote Alexandroúpolis. Were the Greeks really like this?

When I returned that evening Michael was there and handed me a color printout from the Internet with a summary of local history. Athanasios gave me an incredibly strong iced coffee frappé to drink. He also handed me a little brown paper bag with half a dozen publications about regional archeology. They were in Greek, but I could make out some of the titles and look at the maps. He had a two-volume set of paperbacks (illustrated with heroic drawings and color photographs) by Kosta Doika titled: *The Big Secret of Homer* which suggested—another unproved (and doubtful) theory—that Homer was really Odysseus and that the story was autobiographical.

"Did you ever see such a bookstore?" said one of the men who was in our little group. "You won't find any bestsellers here. Only books for specialists and hard thinkers."

The next morning I stopped at the bookstore to buy the two Doika books. "Excuse me, but why are you buying these books if you can't read Greek?" asked a woman who was a local radio and television reporter.

"I like the illustrations," I said, "and hope to learn enough Greek to puzzle my way through the chapter titles and photo captions. I will find a student to translate." The lady shook her head.

Various people in the bookstore told me to visit the museum in Komotini ("early items from Ismarus"). This sounded like a good idea, so Margaret and I rented a tiny Fiat automobile and drove sixty-five kilometers to the northwest. We crossed a low range of coastal mountains and dropped down into the lush green farming country of Thrace. Lovely trees and shrubs bordered the fields. A rainbow of wildflowers grew thickly along the road. It was a beautiful area, and the kilometers flew by.

In Komotini we asked a policeman for directions to the museum, but we couldn't find it. We drove past the crowded downtown, kept bearing right as instructed and worked through a small park that looked vaguely familiar. In desperation we stopped another police-man who turned out to be the first policeman. He looked at us wild-eyed, then smiled and held up a forefinger while he spoke into his portable radio. In a few minutes a police car appeared and led us to the museum. The small museum had excellent displays, and I was thrilled to see a few trinkets and a red clay mask from fourth-century B.C. Maróneia. The mask was a small thing, and it dated from a slightly later time, but it seemed to open a door in my mind to the ancient world. I felt that my story had truly begun. At last we were gaining on Odysseus.

Clay mask of Dionysos.

We drove halfway back to Alexandroúpolis and headed south for the ruins of ancient Maróneia which we learned was the successor to Ismarus. At a sign near the sea we turned off on a dirt road, shifted into first gear, and chugged up a steep track. We stopped at an old shell-shaped Greek theater and poked around some ancient building foundations. High above us on the summit of a nearby coastal mountain were the forbidden Greek radar station and the rubble of the acropolis of Ismarus. The rutted road changed from bad to ghastly as it wound along the steep cliffs above the sea, but the amazing little Fiat kept going. We circled an area of exposed marble, crossed a rocky bluff above a small beach, and stopped at a sign that said "West Wall of Ismarus." I saw a row of tumbledown blocks of stone overgrown with trees. The wall climbed from the sea to the acropolis and according to our guidebook was 4.1 kilometers long.[11]

Earlier I mentioned that Homer wrote how the priest of Apollo—the patron-deity of Ismarus—"gave" Odysseus presents of gold, silver, and fine wine. I can hardly believe that the priest handed over these things voluntarily. Odysseus had a reputation as a raider and a sacker of cities and boasted about it. At Troy he was well-known as a principal officer of the Greeks, who were the enemies of the Cicones. I believe these gifts were a simple payoff to Odysseus not to molest or kidnap for ransom the priest and his family. Can you imagine a priest presenting *gifts* of precious metals and fine wines to an itinerant raider who was killing the priest's people and taking their wives?

Homer understood a basic human truth when he wrote that the strong dominate the weak even though the weak try to improve their lot with flattery, bribes, and service. In modern times, of course, the rule of law helps the weak, but the strong—with their wealth, influence, and superior education—usually prevail.

Ancient Maróneia was founded in 700 B.C. on the ruins of Ismarus by families from the island of Chios. The people raised sheep and cattle and cultivated olive trees, vineyards, and grains. They mined silver and from 520 B.C. onward circulated coins, some of them silver. Not only were there farmers, stockmen, merchants, and mariners, but quarrymen, artisans, potters, and sculptors. In 437 B.C. the population was 12,000. Odysseus didn't know Maróneia, but when he went to Ismarus in 1240 B.C. there must have been parallels.

After hours of jerking and bumping along a track that a camel would have had trouble following, Margaret and I finally escaped and found a paved highway and hurried back to Alexandroúpolis. The next morning we cleared from the port and sailed eighteen miles west to the modern harbor of Maróneia near the ruins we had visited.

Within the boundaries of the Ismarus settlement the ancients constructed a small harbor on the west side of a cape that projects a short distance into the Aegean. The men of old picked a good place, so in 1991, when a modern harbor was built, it was located on the same site. The ancient mole was extended and enlarged, and a seawall was added at the west end. Instead of dredging out the old stones from the innermost part of the harbor, however, they were marked and left in place as a memorial to the ancients.

It seems that Odysseus and his raiders may have tucked his twelve ships behind some of the same stones that Margaret and I tramped over after we sailed into Maróneia harbor and tied up. Odysseus was trying to overpower the Cicones; we were chasing a name and hope. Or had we already succumbed to illusion and fantasy?

Fisherman and sons, Maróneia.

So far we'd seen Troy and Ismarus. Both were small places, but filled with the tracks of real people, people who resisted Odysseus, the man from Ithaca. It took a gutsy warrior to be a leader in the Trojan War. It took a hard driver to be a raider of cities, to arrive in open boats with a gang of thugs and ruffians, and to attack a place with a few bronze spears. Words like independence, fearlessness, and resoluteness fly into my head. Certainly Odysseus was a man who lived on the edge.

A detail from the Akrotiri fresco of 1628 B.C. As far as I know, this is the oldest known drawing of boats and ships. The vessels are similar to later craft except for the curious raised seating arrangement aft of the helmsmen. This one-man post has a seat that's surrounded by a protective outside covering (with a wavy top), an awning, and a person looking around. My guess is that this is a station for the officer of the watch who can see out enough to give orders and perhaps keep track of the course. It appears that a few of the upper class sit comfortably on a raised midships deck (with awning) while the lower class or slaves sweat at the oars below. With a fair wind, the crew will, of course, raise the sail. It seems obvious that craft such as these are suitable for only daylight passages near land and need to stay away from rough seas to keep from filling with water and sinking since they're essentially undecked and not self-righting.

MEN AND SHIPS

S UPPOSE A POWERFUL GOLDEN EAGLE flew upward from Mt. Olympus and circled higher and higher toward the sun. If the royal bird looked down he'd see the Greek peninsula and the Pelopónnisos jutting south into the Mediterranean in the shape of a giant brown hand with three fingers pointing south. From north to south the hand measures 300 miles; east to west 150 miles. East of the hand lies Homer's wine-dark Aegean; west of the hand is the Ionian Sea and Odysseus's home island of Ithaca.

Let's summarize quickly where we are. It was 1240 B.C. The Trojan War was over. The raid against the Cicones in Thrace had begun well but ended in a near disaster. It was time to go home, and Odysseus wanted to return to Ithaca quickly with his men and ships. He missed his small island kingdom, his wife Penelope, and his son. He knew his men were lonely for their families too. But Odysseus was at the wrong end of what we know as present-day Greece. It was centuries before airplanes, trains, or modern roads. The only way was by sea, and these Greek warriors had a long voyage ahead of them.

The distance from Ismarus or modern Maróneia at the northeast corner of the Aegean Sea to Ithaca via Cape Malea is about 565 nautical miles if measured in straight-line sailing distances around the U-shaped Pelopónnisos. However the sailors of ancient times seldom elected direct sea passages. They almost always chose safer, zigzag routes from island to island or along known coastlines rather than across the open sea. Without compasses and charts the sailors had to navigate by memory, the angle of the sun or stars at certain hours, or—more likely—by hope and wishful thinking.

The fighting ships of old had no cooking or formal sleeping arrangements for their large crews. The men stopped on land for rest and nourishment and waited for reasonable weather, which generally meant a fair wind so they could use the sails. The summer wind from the north—the meltemi—often blew up to thirty or thirty-five knots and caused a rough sea with wave crests of two or three meters in exposed places. The fighting ships of the ancients were undecked and had low freeboard; even a small breaking sea could swamp a ship in a twinkling. Then, in spite of frantic last-chance bailing, it was all over. The survivors, if any, tended to be more conservative in their subsequent sailing and the hand-me-down knowledge they passed on. Sailors hate to take chances and risk everything. Instead they play the conservative game so they will be alive tomorrow.

The distance from Ismarus to Ithaca via the islands is about 665 miles—100 miles longer than the straight-line route. If we assume that Odysseus sailed for ten hours a day and averaged three knots, then the Ithaca-bound trip would have taken about three weeks. In sea-going missions with large numbers of men and ships of any kind, however, delays are usual and expected and would have been caused by:

- EQUIPMENT FAILURES—broken oars, stove-in hulls from dragging the ships up rocky beaches.
- FOOD SHORTAGES—the men had some dried rations, but were largely living off the land as they went along.
- CREW PROBLEMS—bickering, splitting up booty, and arguing about additional raids although since everyone was headed home these disagreements would have been minimal.

I keep writing "Odysseus and his men," but how many fighters did he have when he left Ismarus? Homer gives few numbers in his story. Certainly during the ten-year Trojan war, combat casualties and disease would have cut the original fighting force from Ithaca. Others in Odysseus's group must have deserted or died from accidents or natural causes. How many men were left? An optimistic figure would be ninety percent of the original force. We know that Odysseus had twelve sleek fighting ships. What does this tell us about crew requirements?

Except for one tiny Bronze Age merchantman—circa 1200 B.C.—that was recovered from the sea bottom at Turkey's Cape Gelidonya by George Bass and a group of divers in 1960, archeologists have found almost no hard evidence of ancient ship design. No one really knows how many men an open warship carried. What little evidence there is comes from vase paintings, bits of sculpture, coins, seals, and a few other spotty clues.[12]

In 1974—just a few years ago—a number of wonderful paintings were discovered under layers of volcanic ash on the Greek island of Thera in the southwestern Aegean. It was long thought that the huge volcanic explosion that dumped tons of ash and pumice on the ancient village of Akrotiri and elsewhere in the region occurred around 1550 B.C. Recently scientists have used tree-ring dating to find the exact time of the eruption. The annual growth rings on the trunk or branch of a tree vary according to wet and dry cycles and act as precise fingerprints for climate, weather, and dating. By using this technique on timbers found in the village the date of the eruption was found to be 1628 B.C.

The eruption and weight of the pumice collapsed the buildings of the village and partially ruined a series of frescoes on some of the walls of the houses. Yet the dry pumice preserved the fragments until the paintings were found and miraculously restored. Made about 228 years before the Trojan War (plus the age of the paintings before their inundation), this remarkable window to the past shows full-figured women with surprisingly modern clothing and jewelry, fishermen, boys boxing, warriors with shields, dolphins, swallows, and graceful antelopes, all executed in a decorative, embellished style. One colorful mural details seven ships of the time with 70-foot hull profiles, oarsmen, helmsmen using steering oars, and sails and rigging that could have been used by Odysseus.[13]

We know there were two kinds of ships in the fleet at Troy, the twenty-oared and the fifty-oared. Each vessel was built from a series of U-shaped frames that were erected across and along a stout keel timber almost the length of the ship. Longitudinal planks were then fitted around this structure. As the planking proceeded, the shipwrights cut matching hollows (mortises) in the planks every few feet and fitted protruding hardwood pieces (tenons) that led vertically from one plank to another. Gradually the builders extended the planking into wide, strong, curved sides. The planking was fastened to the frames with hardwood pegs called trenails that were driven into place. Sometimes the frames were added after the planks; other times the frames—or partial frames—were erected first. The details are unknown because descriptive writing was only in a formative stage and certainly not a concern of ancient boatbuilders whose superiors may have wished to keep their building procedures secret in any case. [14]

The end result was a smooth, sleek carvel-planked hull with a long, flat sheer. Often the bow and sometimes the stern were swept upward in high, dramatic curves. The hull was then smeared with pitch for watertightness and launched. It floated on the surface with the keel downward because of the barge-like shape of the hull sections and the weight of the live ballast of men and their gear. If inclined more than a certain angle, however, the boat would capsize and fill with water.

The waterproofing pitch made the ships black, but the builders fastened flashy decorations of yellow, red, or blue at the prows. Meanwhile shipwrights hewed stout masts and yards from solid wood. Carpenters fashioned oars by the hundreds. Two-strand ropes—which sailors call fox lay—were twisted from vegetable fibers. Other cordage was plaited from strips of leather. Patient weavers fashioned flax into sail fabric on small looms, and sailmakers sewed the squares and rectangles of cloth into the great white panels that would drive the ships.

The twenty-oared vessel must have been at least fifty-five feet long because each oarsman or pair of oarsmen needed three and a half feet or a little more. Ten men on a side added up to thirty-five feet, plus ten feet each for the curved bow and stern. Homer mentions that the ships were seven feet wide near the stern where the helmsman handled the steering oar, so these war canoes must have been nine or ten feet wide amidships. It seems likely that the ancient warships were ballasted with a few stones to increase their stability although they were light enough to be run up on any convenient beach. Later in the story Odysseus was able to shove his boat free of the land with a single thrust of a boat pole when he was in a rush to get away from the island of the Cyclops.

I've seen the long, slim, open wooden boats used by modern whalers in the Azores in the Atlantic until whaling was outlawed a few years ago. The boats of Odysseus must have been similar except the craft of the ancient Greeks were longer, beamier, and probably a little more stoutly built. A basic requirement of the modern whalers was that each man in the crew had to sit in the middle of his position and sit still. He pulled hard on his oar, and he didn't move around. The whaling boats were delicate, and when taken out of the water I've watched the Portuguese sailors carefully prop up and support the hulls with boards and sticks to keep the hot sun from warping the thin wooden structures. The whalers stayed on shore in bad weather, didn't go out at night, and took every prudent action to stay out of trouble.

Homer refers to his ships as "hollow" which means undecked. Any chop or waves slopped over the sides, especially when going to windward, so spray shields were rigged at the bow to divert green water. To help protect the thin planking from inside damage and to spread the weight of the mast and gear, pieces of brush were cut and fitted inside the hull. A crude anchor, provisions, jars of water, clothing, weapons, body armor, helmets, booty, personal items, and oars were stowed under the partial decks and rowing seats.

Whether all the oarsmen were used at the same time or in two shifts is unknown. You can argue each way: two on an oar to go faster or one man to spell another. However the extra oarsmen had to be fed and supervised, and their weight was certainly a factor. In any case, fifty or sixty temperamental Greeks penned up on one of these narrow cockleshells for long periods must have demanded rigid discipline and stern officers at times. No wonder the ships tried to make short runs from one place to another.

The concept of galley slaves who were chained to their benches and subject to brutal labor, horrific discipline, and who lived under appalling conditions came much later. The galley slave belongs to medieval naval warfare of the sixteenth and seventeenth centuries A.D., not to the Greek period of long ago. The crews of the warships of Homer's era that we're talking about were made up of free men who were fighters, companions, and volunteers from Ithaca, Kefallenía, and Zákinthos. They sailed when possible and rowed when there was no wind or a light contrary wind. They fought as a unit and divided spoils from the enemy.

But back to the number of crewmen. Homer gives us a clue when he writes about Circe's Isle in Book Ten of *The Odyssey*. There he speaks of dividing the ship's company into two groups of twenty-two. So at that time the ship's crew totaled only forty-four men since six had been lost in the attack on Ismarus and six during the episode with the Cyclops on Sicily. Working backwards, therefore, and allowing a modest ten-percent shrinkage for casualties, desertions, and losses from disease, accidents, and natural causes, the full crew of a twenty-oared warship starting out from Ithaca might have looked like this:

        20 rowers
        24 relief rowers
         2 helmsmen
         2 lookouts
         2 mates
         1 captain
         8 fighting marines
         2 ship's boys
        ─────────
        61

The fifty-oared ship was similar to the twenty-oared but longer, probably one hundred feet or more, and of course beamier. The corresponding numbers for the larger vessel are:

        50 rowers
        50 relief rowers
         3 helmsmen
         3 lookouts
         2 mates
         1 captain
        12 fighting marines
         3 ship's boys
        ─────────
        124

Later, after I worked all this out, I discovered two lines in *The Iliad* (Fagles, book 2, 598–9):

> Fifty ships came freighted with these contingents
> One hundred twenty young Boeotians manning each.

So my numbers may be reasonable even though one authority believes that my estimates are too high.

The totals for twelve of the twenty-oared ships are 732. For the fifty-oared ships 1,488 men. On an expedition of this size the captain must have taken say three shipwrights, three sailmakers, three armorers, and a religious person, perhaps ten specialists. This would raise the totals to 742 and 1,498. The kingdom of Ithaca was small and poor compared with the rich centers of Mycenae, Pylos, and Tiryns, and we know that Odysseus was a grudging contributor. Therefore I believe he came to Troy with twelve of the twenty-oared ships and 742 men. After the Trojan war his force was ten percent less or about 668 men.

When Odysseus left Ismarus he had this group minus the 72 casualties from the fighting with the Cicones or 596. However he must have taken a few women along because Homer mentioned dividing up both the wives and rich plunder when he raided Ismarus. Add another twenty to the total.

My final figure is that Odysseus sailed south from Ismarus with twelve ships and 616 people.

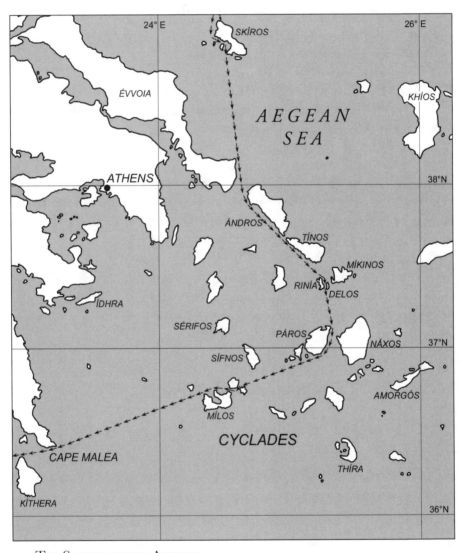

THE SOUTHWESTERN AEGEAN

SOUTH
IN THE AEGEAN

A
S WE'VE SEEN, Odysseus and his party fled from Ismarus
with heavy hearts because the relief they felt at their escape was countered by grief for their comrades who had
been killed by the Cicones. With hindsight the men knew they
should have slipped away earlier before the reinforced enemy
attacked. They realized they were lucky to escape death themselves and were glad to climb into their ships, pull at the long
oars, and watch the coast of Thrace fade into the distance.

Some raids were successful; others were not. Certainly with
seventy-two deaths the Ismarus raid was a failure. Pirates and
raiders and soldiers expect casualties when they inflict barbari-
ties on a peaceful community, but losses of eleven percent must
have shocked Odysseus. It reflects badly on the supposed great
leader who early on had ordered his men to leave but failed to
follow up on his directive. Now, however, the episode was over.
It was time to head south for Cape Malea and home.

Homer, writing as Odysseus, said:

> Next Zeus, the cloud-marshal, incited against our fleet a North
> wind, with screaming squalls. He blinded land and sea alike
> with clouds. Night plunged down from heaven. The ships were
> swept aside before the blast and their sails shredded into tat-
> ters by the gale. We had to strike them in instant fear of death,
> and take to the oars. Vehemently we tugged our ships shore-
> ward. For two days and two nights we lay there, making no way

and eating our hearts out with despair and the unceasing labour: but on the third morning bright-haired Dawn achieved clear daylight; wherefore up went our masts and white shining sails, enabling us to sit there at our ease watching how the winds and the steersmen held us to our course.[15]

Homer is silent on the route of the ships, but after the battle, the fighting, and the frantic escape from Ismarus, the twelve ships would have been wildly disorganized. My guess is they headed for the island of Samothráki, a run of only twenty-one miles to the south and a place that's easy to find and land on. Once there the leaders would have assigned some of the men to steal cattle and sheep from the local people. Others would have then butchered and grilled the animals. The meat would have been used for ritual sacrifice and to feed the six-hundred-odd hungry raiders. Meanwhile the men could have caught their breath, regrouped, no doubt made a few repairs to the ships, and adjusted their leadership arrangements after the bloody battle in Ismarus.

The next morning the twelve ships would have left the pleasant north coast of Samothráki. However Odysseus didn't allow the fleet to sail until each of the men who had been killed in the fighting had been saluted three times. Then the great war canoes swept out to sea and gradually turned south-southwest for Limnos, fifty miles away, keeping the rising sun on their port hand. Partway along, a northerly wind sprang up, and the ships hurried before it. The sailors were happy with the fair wind, and late in the day they coasted past the five high mountains on the west coast of Limnos.

But the sky turned gray and dark. Low, blustery clouds swept over the sea. Wind roared down from their ragged edges and began to pummel the fleet. The smiles of the sailors changed to nervous frowns. As the black night fell, the wind increased even more. Waves began to build up, and in a few hours a great northerly gale was blowing. The ocean was vast; the matchstick fleet was tiny and exposed; the ships raced before the wind. Here and there the linen squaresails began to rip and tear. During the long night the frantic sailors clawed down the torn sails, lowered the yards, and unstepped the masts. As soon as it was light, Odysseus scanned the sea. He saw land ahead to port and recognized the familiar brown hills and mountains of Skíros, which he knew from his visit when he'd recruited Achilles for the Trojan War. The wind was still strong and the seas nasty, but by using the oars the fleet was able to work crabwise across the waves. Soon the Greek sailors were pulling like madmen for the land.

Unlike modern sailors who look for sheltered bays protected from the wind and sea in order to anchor, the ancients didn't fear exposed lee shores. The Greeks headed for the nearest shelving beach and rowed until they touched bottom. Then everyone jumped into the water, grabbed hold of the ship, and ran the vessel up on the beach out of reach of the waves. The men on the first boat then hurried back into the sea to help the others. Soon all twelve ships were high and dry. But the men were exhausted. Their spirits had collapsed. Was the trip back to Ithaca going to be like this all the way? How could they possibly survive? The sea would kill them.

The shipwrights began to check the hulls, and the sailmakers set to work to repair all twelve sails of the fleet, a big sewing job. Meanwhile a party was sent to scout for food. The fleet had come two jumps south from Samothráki—a hundred and twenty-five miles in two days. At this rate, going home would be quick—if they didn't perish on the way.

From Linaria and Port Trebuki on the south side of Skíros it's easy to see the long row of mountains on Euboea to the southwest. Euboea (yoo-BEE-a) is ninety miles long and so large that many consider it part of mainland Greece. Certainly some of Odysseus's men would have recognized its bumpy skyline.

On the third morning the dawn was clear and bright. The big wind and dark clouds had vanished. The sailmakers had done their work, and the men were impatient. Odysseus decided to go to Delos to pray at the temple of Apollo. Why not? Delos was only a little out of the way. It would be good for everyone, and with Apollo's help the trip home might be safer and easier.

The fleet sailed south from Skíros for the channel between Euboea and Ándros, fifty-two miles ahead. During the summer the meltemi, the powerful wind from the north, blows hard in this region and sets up a strong south-flowing current in the channel—Stenón Kafirévs. Then the strait is rough and turbulent and dotted with overfalls and breaking seas. Even today the British Admiralty prints a prominent warning about the strait on its chart 1087. The crews of small, fully-decked modern vessels sometimes have their hands full trying to stay out of trouble.

Odysseus and the ships passed safely through the strait and coasted southeastward for another forty-eight miles along the shores of Ándros, Tínos, and Míkonos to Delos, a tiny island between Míkonos and Rinía. Delos is only five kilometers long from north to south and 1,300 meters wide, but to the ancient Greeks it was the center of the world, the hub of the universe, the heart and soul of their spiritual empire.

We know that either on this voyage or during a previous one Odysseus stopped at Delos, worshipped at an early temple of Apollo, and spoke of his amazement at the sight of a perfectly formed young palm tree sprouting up next to the altar. It seems reasonable that the leader of a group of fighting men returning victorious from a long and difficult war would have stopped at this sacred island for a few days. The officers and men would have offered prayers and sprinkled barley grains; they would have slaughtered and ritually burnt parts of sheep and cattle; they would have poured libations of wine, burned incense, and sung and danced to religious melodies, all with the hope of influencing the gods in their favor.

The men from Ithaca would have behaved themselves. They wouldn't have dreamed of raiding sacred Delos for food. Odysseus would have used some of his gold to buy what he needed. Or he may have been more deliberate and calculating: he couldn't afford to take chances. It would have been stupid to insult a god in a sacred place. Who knew when you might need that god's help?[16]

From Delos the next move (fifty-seven miles) would have been to Milos (right on course, prominent, with good stopping places). Then to Cape Malea (sixty-one miles), the southernmost point of mainland Greece.

Cape Malea (pronounced ma-LEE-a) was the Cape Horn of the ancients, the home of myths and fanciful legends; the terrible place where violent winds and turbulent seas caused shipwrecks and mysterious disappearances. The ancient sailors had a

This statue of Apollo is from Olympia, but similar figures were in the temples to Apollo on Delos.

saying: "Round Malea and forget your native country," but now the fleet was bound for home. If the ships could slip by Malea and the other two fingers of the Pelopónnisos they would be in the familiar Ionian Sea. Their home islands were then "just over the horizon" to the northwest.

As capes go, Malea doesn't amount to much, but it's significant weather-wise. This bold and mountainous headland is less than 2,000 feet high, but rounding it is always a thrill because you pass from the Aegean into the main waters of the Mediterranean. In the summer you exchange the northerly winds of the meltemi for often persistent westerlies, but any sort of wind can blow—or not blow. In centuries past, tens of thousands of ships have struggled past this place: In 200 A.D. it was 180-foot sailing freighters from

Rome that carried as much as 1,300 tons of Egyptian grain in a single load. Nearby Vatica bay was long a stopping place for Roman and Venetian galleys. In the 17th and 18th centuries ships from England and Venetian three-masters more than 200 feet long passed on their way to the Levant or Alexandria. Generally it was easy as far as Malea; then the baffling winds began. This Greek cape was once a place where pirates lurked. Dozens of large and small sea battles have been fought in its shadow. During World Wars I and II, British and German patrol ships traded shells and positions, and the crews crept ashore at night to bury their dead.[17]

But our focus is 1,250 B.C. when Odysseus and his toothpick fleet of twelve reached Malea. The fleet hoped to head westward and home, but the sea and wind had other ideas.

Odysseus said:

> I should have reached my own land safe and sound, had not the swell, the current, and the North Wind combined, as I was doubling Malea, to drive me off my course and send me drifting past Cythera. For nine days I was chased by those accursed winds across the fish-infested seas.[18]

The fleet tried to sail west, but the wind and current pushed them south. The sailors watched in dismay as the shores of Cythera—now called Kithera—fell away to port. Soon the fair land of Greece disappeared entirely, and the men from Ithaca were in waters completely unknown to them. Odysseus had no idea what was south and west. On a previous voyage he had sailed downwind to Egypt (south and east) and had averaged three knots or about seventy-two miles a day.

On and on the six hundred sailors went, never seeing other ships, wondering if they would ever walk through their homes again, play with their children, or make love to their wives. They stared at the hard blue line of the horizon, three miles away. They looked at endless whitecaps from the northwest. They felt seawater swirl around their feet, and they leaned over to fill the clay bailing pots. Fill and dump. Fill and dump. Fill and dump. . . .

They had started out with jars—amphorae—topped up with drinking water. Other jars held concentrated wine from Ismarus. But wine is no good at sea on empty stomachs. What sailors need is water, particularly in the heat of summer when men drink a lot. But how long would it last? Most of the fruit was bruised and had gone rotten, but they had olives and chewed dried meat and dried fish and ate onions, cheese, and shellfish.

Day after day the strong wind whistled past their ears. The north wind gradually veered to the east, but they only vaguely realized it when the sun was low in the sky in the morning or evening. Usually the sun burned down, but sometimes their bodies felt the relief of clouds. Even though it was summer the nights were cool, and they often experienced a chill before dawn.

The sea grew warmer. When they looked toward the south the sky seemed whiter, with a crystalline brilliance. Odysseus didn't know it, but the whiteness, the brightness, came from the reflected sand and baked earth of the Sahara and the desert lands of Africa along the coast to the south.

By the end of the ninth day they had traveled more than seven hundred miles in a great curving arc. Initially—with north and northeast winds behind them—they sailed south and a little west from Malea almost to the coast of Africa. The arc of their course then curved westward across the Gulf of Sidra and the coast of Tripolitania as the Greek fleet paralleled the African coast and experienced easterly winds.

Finally the arc turned a little northwest—again paralleling the curve of the African coast—as the coast sweeps northward toward Cape Bon. Now the ragtag fleet found southeast winds because every day the diamond-bright sun beats down on the north-south coastal desert plain of Tunisia to the west. The rising hot air sucks air from the Mediterranean to the east. Hence the easterly flow of wind.

Most—or at least many—students of Homer believe the twelve ships wound up in Djerba. (The direct distance from Cape Malea to the Houmt Souk harbor entrance is 627 miles on a course of 255°). If we use Homer's figure of an average rate of three knots and calculate (3 knots x 24 hours x 9 days) we get 648 miles, only 50 miles short of the estimated 700 miles that Odysseus sailed on his south-curving voyage to the Djerba (see endpaper map). We can easily explain the missing 50 miles by allowing for and east-setting current of 1/4 know set up by the fair wind. Of course the sailors had no idea how far they'd come because they lacked timepieces, nautical charts, and a way to gauge the speed of their ships.

The late Ernle Bradford pointed out that both Herodotus (fifth century B.C.) and Scylax of Caryanda (writing in 350 B.C.)—who were both reasonable witnesses of the ancient scene—identified Djerba as the destination of the fleet. At least their arguments have the weight of contemporary thinking because they lived within a few centuries of Homer.

For every mile Odysseus & Co. sailed south they traveled three miles west. The wind now had a regular pattern: In the mornings it blew from the northeast. Around noon it veered to the east, and in the early afternoon began to blow from the southeast and often continued all night. There would then be a few hours of calm before the cycle started again. These winds and the wind-induced current combined to push the fleet past western Libya into what is now Tunisia and toward a small island just off the African coast.[19]

The brisk wind, which is southeast in this region, grew lighter. Broken clouds lay at mid-altitude, and the swell was less. The horizon ahead and to the south had a different sparkle to it, and some of the men felt sure of a change. It was a miracle, but the twelve ships were still together. Two had leaked, but their crews plugged the seams and kept up. One of the captains heard a squeaking noise. The men looked up at two small land birds flitting past. On the morning of the tenth day the color of the water was different. No longer was the sea a dark blue-black. It was more greenish and shallow. Now the men could see the bottom. Everyone looked over the side at sand, grass, rocks, and fish. There was a shout and a gesture from the leading ship. Ahead lay the dim brown of a land none of the men had ever seen before. It was Djerba, a little more than 600 miles from Cape Malea.

Sailing south toward Samothráki.

THE LONG ROUTE
TO AFRICA

MARGARET AND I SAILED from Maróneia in mid-summer. The sky was the color of blue silk, and a light northerly breeze danced down the steep shoreline mountains of Thrace and filled our sails. In the south we could see the cone of Samothráki rising from a sapphire sea and disappearing into the clouds. Again on the trail of Odysseus, we started on the long track to Africa.

We took turns steering *Whisper*, and in a little over five hours we glided into the main port of Kamariotissa, a dreary place choked with junky tourist shops from one end to the other. It had the charm of a county jail.

We rented a motorbike and traveled along the north side of the island. Once away from the port, the island was beautiful. We thought the remote northeast corner at the end of the road would have been a good place to have beached the twelve ships of Odysseus because there's a long shelving beach, trees for firewood, and the Fonias river, a lovely freshwater stream that flows northeastward into the sea. Sheep and cattle from the ancient settlement of Paleopoli probably roamed the hills in 1200 B.C. The area was close to Ismarus and in settled weather would have been an easy and obvious goal for the weary warriors. It was at Paleopoli in 1863 where a Frenchman named Charles Champoiseau found the famous statue of the Winged Victory of Samothrace, now in the Louvre museum in Paris.

From Samothráki we sailed overnight to Skíros, 116 miles to the south-southwest, passing the big island of Limnos. We chose an anchorage on the south shore, but we had the greatest trouble getting our anchor to hold in the thick grass on the seabed of Linaria cove. We tried the CQR anchor three times. Then a Danforth anchor twice. Finally we assembled our 30-kilo Luke storm anchor (a Herreshoff fisherman pattern) which cut through the weed on the first try. But the effort took an hour and a half, and I was puffing mightily after cranking up 50 meters of chain five times.

For the next four days the north wind blew hard, and we were delighted to stay anchored in Linaria cove while the meltemi whistled overhead. Each day we walked to the nearby village of Linaria to buy fresh bread, fruit, and vegetables. On the nearby beach we made friends with a taverna owner who died laughing at our attempts to speak Greek from a phrase book. We met the postmistress in Linaria who sorted through her stamps to give us pretty ones to paste on our letters. From the cliffs above the beach we looked southwest across twenty-five miles of the Aegean to the mountains on Euboea.

The wind eased off on the morning of the fifth day. I was impatient to move on, so we pulled up our anchor and headed for Delos. We started in light winds, but the meltemi began to blow hard again. We put up our running rig and soon *Whisper* was rush-

The pleasant village of Linaria on the south coast of Skiros is tucked in a bay within a bay and is well protected from the meltemi wind.

ing along at a steady seven knots, which is fast for a small vessel. By the late afternoon, reefed down and with a lot of water flying around, we had logged sixty miles in eight hours with one knot of current behind us.

We stopped overnight at the port of Gavrion on the northwest corner of Ándros and early the next morning again hurried southwest toward Delos. The bulk of the big island of Ándros now protected us from the strong north wind, but when we cleared the island and began sailing along the southwest side of Tínos great squalls began to blast down on *Whisper.*

[FROM THE LOG] 19 June. 1900 hours. We're anchored off a beach about 1½ miles northwest of the main harbor of Tínos. It was a long afternoon. To recap: The wind picked up after passing the gap between Ándros and Tínos. Before that the wind was spotty so I shook out the third reef. For a time we sailed with the full jib and two reefs, but the wind grew stronger and stronger. I soon rolled up the jib entirely. We bashed along with the main with two reefs but needed a third. We were near the harbor of Tínos, however, and I thought we could make it without another reef. As we approached the port the wind rose to 43 knots on the meter, and I realized it would be impossible to maneuver in the harbor. I spotted a long shelving beach to windward that looked like a possible anchorage. We took a couple of tacks to get closer. Fortunately the yacht tacks well (but slowly) with the mainsail alone. I was worried about rocks off the beach, but suddenly through the spray I saw a fishing boat motoring along just off the beach. No rocks! As we went in, the waves grew less and less. We anchored in four meters in sand. I let go 20 meters of chain, and the anchor bit in at once with a big jerk. The mainsail was flogging violently, but we gradually pulled it down and tamed it with ties. I see that the #2 reefing pendant is broken. Summer sailing in Greece. Bah!

Two days later the strong winds vanished, and we sailed the ten miles to Delos in trifling airs. As we ghosted along at a knot or two under full sail in the narrow channel between Rinía and Delos we looked to our right at treeless, deserted, sun-baked Rinía with its ancient stone fences that circled old farming sites and vineyards and pastures. Where had the descendants of the thousands who had once lived there gone? One thing was certain: there must have been more trees and topsoil and moisture in the old days because the bleak and sterile slopes of modern-day Rinía would have trouble supporting a hundred people. I couldn't help but think of too many people on a small island farming too hard and cutting too many trees. Of erosion, failed crops, deforestation, silted harbors, little fresh water—a dreadful pattern that destroyed their future.

To our left lay the tiny sliver of Delos, another sun-baked desert rockpile that was once the political and commercial center of the Aegean. In Greek mythology the islet was the birthplace of Apollo and Artemis, and the spiritual heart of the ancient world. The island had special temples with enormous stone figures, and it was here that the Oracle of Delos delivered his decisions. It was forbidden to die on Delos, to be buried there, or for a woman to give birth to a child. People on their last gasp were whisked across to Rinía, as were women about to deliver.

According to historians, the ancient Greeks and later the Romans turned Delos into a great trading crossroads for grain and a

Who, I wondered, was the man who chiseled these letters on this granite block among the temple ruins? How and when did he do it? What sort of a man was he? The inscription reads: Απολλο (capital A plus five lower-case Greek letters) or Apollo in English.

financial center for banking and insurance. The island was prominent in the slave trade, and as many as 10,000 slaves were traded or sold in a single day. These figures are repeated in many books, and there's much talk about the great commercial port of olden times. In 88 B.C. Mithridates VI sacked the island.[20]

Could these facts be exaggerated? Could a few historians be guilty of copying? One from the other? Certainly the present-day artificial harbor is small, shallow, and poor. The approaches are dangerous in strong winds, and the tiny island (five kilometers long and 1300 meters wide) has nothing at all in the way of natural resources. In any case by 200 A.D. the island was abandoned.

We went ashore to see this famous Greek monument. Along with hundreds of tourists brought by excursion boats from Míkonos and Náxos we bought entrance tickets and a guidebook and walked into a large area of tumbled-down ruins. Everywhere we saw the drums of columns, broken pillars of marble, mutilated, weathered statues, and massive foundations of dead temples that were pulled down long ago. Delos has been plundered for centuries: first by the Isaurians, the Slavs, the Saracens, and by pirates. Then by the Venetians, the Knights of St. John of Malta, and by the Turks. Much of its marble was crushed for building purposes. The bronze cramps

*Ruins of a temple to Apollo on Delos. The barren island of
Rinía is in the distance.*

that held the blocks of stone together in ancient times were pried
out and melted down long ago.

In later years Delos was ravaged by travelers from England,
France, Italy, Holland, and most of all by the Greeks who treated
the place as a handy stone quarry for the nearby islands. Most of
the good relics are in private hands or in national museums in
London, Paris, Berlin, or Athens, and there's little left of value on
the island. French archeologists have worked on the island since

1872 and continue their commendable efforts, but it must take a dedicated scientist to work on such a devastated site. Today's Greeks realize the value of Delos as a tourist attraction and attempt to guard and preserve the island, but it's not much use locking the bank after the gold is gone.

My main interest was a temple to Apollo. However no temples of the sort we think of as classical Greek existed on Delos in Mycenaean times (1200 B.C.). But our story says that Odysseus stopped at Delos and mentions Apollo's altar and a tiny palm shoot growing alongside. The altar must have been in some kind of a building, probably with an earthen floor, a forerunner to the large, marble, columnar structures that we know. New temples are often built on the ruins of the old, and we must have been on historic grounds because our guidebook mentioned "the ruins of three temples to Apollo standing in a line."

The guidebook to Delos described a later temple in glowing terms and showed an artist's drawing, but it's based on guesswork, and in truth all that's left is a massive weed-choked, dusty foundation and a few shattered stones and columns—a pitiful relic.

The last statue of Apollo was said to have been four times life size. An artist named S. de Vries made a drawing of two parts of it (the head and the trunk) in 1673, but the head was carted off long ago.[21]

The place was a great disappointment.

FROM DELOS WE CONTINUED SOUTHWEST and stopped at a lovely anchorage on the west side of uninhabited Políaigos island in the complex of islands around Mílos. I wanted to pass Cape Malea during the day so I could see it and watch out for the heavy shipping traffic that flows by this easternmost branch of the Pelopónnisos. Accordingly, the next day we left in the late afternoon, sailed seventy miles, and reached the cape the following morning.

By 0900 we were two miles from the steep slopes of Cape Malea and were re-living the dreams of all the mariners who had preceded us. Had Odysseus passed this way in daylight? Were there initially calms and then a howling northeaster that blew his fleet before it?

As we passed this southern point of mainland Greece we sailed into a headwind from the west-southwest, just the direction we wanted to go. In a twinkling we were heeled to twenty knots of wind. Our best heading was south, and we soon became aware of an east-setting current from compass bearings on Kíthera island south of us. There seemed little point in bashing against an adverse wind and current, so we anchored in the lee of an islet near the easternmost point of Kíthera. The next morning the wind was a little less, so we sailed to the north point of Kíthera and once clear of the island tacked to the south-southwest. A lee shore lay on our port hand, but we knew the current would be less, and we were soon clear of the island. Now our route was clear all the way to Djerba.

The next six days passed quickly. Margaret and I stood watch and watch and kept a careful lookout for merchant ships, tankers, and fishing boats. We stood watches of three or four hours and slept in rotation until we accumulated six or seven hours of sleep in twenty-four. We had winds mostly from the northwest, southwest, and south, and only two hours of calms.

We ate well. We had bought juicy oranges, vine-ripened tomatoes, bunches of shimmering green grapes, and yellow apples in Greece. We had several green summer melons whose sweet taste would have tempted Saint Anthony. My favorite dish was fried slices of fresh eggplant (dipped in beaten egg and bread crumbs seasoned with salt and pepper and Parmesan cheese). We still had a few bottles of Turkish red wine, and a glass or two of Güzel Marmara was pleasant at dusk.

On July 21st it breezed up to twenty-eight knots from the west, so we hove to for thirteen hours and slowly moved toward the south-southwest. Once a big eastbound oil tanker, a VLCC (a very large crude carrier) came close to us at noon. We hoped she would change course a little because we were hard-pressed, but she thundered past us only 100 meters away while the officer on watch calmly studied us with his binoculars. She was monstrous and scary and after she passed, it took me an hour to calm down. A few hours later the wind eased and we got underway.

We hadn't seen many large fish in the Aegean, probably because of gross over-fishing. Now that we were in the wide open

Margaret steering Whisper *past Cape Malea, a surprisingly small place where shipping lanes meet and the weather often changes abruptly.*

*Entrance buoy to the three-mile dredged channel
to Houmt Souk, Djerba. The buoy shows the
usual signs: bird droppings and a bent frame
from being slammed about by ships which are
forever running into buoys. This one looks old-
fashioned but sports two solar panels to power
the light.*

spaces of the Mediterranean and a hundred miles or more from
land we sometimes saw schools of tuna—a meter or more long—
rushing after tiny silvery fish. The small fish would thrash around
at the surface while the tuna beat the water white while they fed.
Birds (how do they know?) invariably appeared and rushed to the
scene and dived into the foaming circle. This went on for ten
minutes or so until it suddenly ended. The birds, no doubt disappointed, then slowly flew away. If we changed course to sail to
the tuna, the surface feeding was generally over by the time we
arrived. Once after a feeding episode, a school of tuna rushed
past us at great speed. The sun glinted on their silver and blue

and yellow bodies, a vision of power and speed and beauty. In the few seconds while I peered into the sea I thought of a camera (below in the cabin) and a fishing line (not ready). Then-snap!- the fish were gone. The only thing left was the memory of their lovely muscular bodies, their metallic colors, and how they swam so close and fast without bumping one another.

Finally we neared Libya and Tunisia and sailed into a corner of the Mediterranean that was new to us. Most of this great sea is tideless, but in the southern portion there's a significant rise and fall of the water.

> [FROM THE LOG] 23 July. 2027 hours. This part of the Mediter-
> ranean has a much different feel than the Aegean or the Ionian
> because of the clouds. Just now the sun is setting behind a mid-
> altitude swath of ragged altocumulus, and is bathing the sea in
> a soft, beautiful light. We're about sixty miles from land, but
> the clouds to the west suggest different temperatures and
> weather. During the summer there are few clouds in the rainless
> Mediterranean. In the south, however, we're seeing cumulus,
> stratus, and alto-cumulus, particularly in the early morning.

Each day it had grown warmer—it was up to 30 or 32°C. [90°F.] in the cabin—and the sun blasted down. At sea the horizon is generally a hard, distinct line of blue between the sky and sea; now in the south, however, the line grew indistinct. The southern sky was white, diamond-bright, and hard to look at without squinting; we were seeing the reflected light of the African desert. The sea was shallower now, absolutely calm without swell, and the color of the water changed from a deep inky-blue to dark turquoise, then to shades of green. Sometimes we could see the bottom, which was a shock. Small terns with long forked tails rushed around the yacht, their screeching calls slicing through the air.

A little after noon on July 24th we saw a thin strip of land to the south. We were sailing well with an easterly wind, and under a reefed genoa we glided down the narrow four-mile dredged en-trance channel to Houmt Souk, the main port of Djerba. Not counting tacking, we had come 1,007 miles from Marónia in Thrace.

Fishing boats with lateen rigs, Houmt Souk.

LAND OF
THE LOTUS-EATERS

Odysseus said:

> I sent some of my followers inland to find out what sort of human beings might be there, detailing two men for the duty with a third as a messenger. Off they went, and it was not long before they were in touch with the Lotus-eaters. Now it never entered the heads of these natives to kill my friends; what they did was to give them some lotus to taste, and as soon as each had eaten the honeyed fruit of the plant, all thoughts of reporting to us or escaping were banished from his mind. All they now wished for was to stay where they were with the Lotus-eaters, to browse on the lotus and to forget that they had a home to return to. I had to use force to bring them back to the ships, and they wept on the way.[22]

MARGARET AND I SAILED into the main port of Houmt Souk on the north coast of Djerba at 1530 on July 24th. We tied up near an old square-towered fort called Bordj el K'bir. The main port sounds like a big deal, but in truth Houmt Souk was an ancient, tiny, shallow fishing boat harbor without potable water, electricity, or very much room. There was the usual smell of fish, and all around us the dark-skinned south Tunisians chatted away in harsh-vowelled, staccato Arabic as they stopped to look at the strange yacht from America.

Not many people have heard of Djerba. It's a small island—

roughly fifteen miles by fifteen miles. It's just offshore in southern Tunisia and is about forty-five miles northwest of the Libyan border. This low, flat African island has a population of 115,000 and is part of the Sahara desert with scorching daily temperatures; yet it's surrounded by the Mediterranean, has long white beaches, date palms, olive trees, and lots of market garden produce. The heat is mitigated by cool sea breezes from the east but almost everyone—locals and tourists alike—carries a small bottle of spring water and takes sips all day long.

Although the latitude was 33°53' north, we had to wear shoes because we could have fried eggs on the deck. We quickly put up our awning over *Whisper's* main boom, and the patch of shade was wonderful. Fortunately there was a steady breeze across the harbor which had about forty large and small wooden vessels. Most were powered by one-cylinder diesel engines, but there were a dozen or so that used the lateen rig and gray cotton sails. A main business in Houmt Souk is octopus fishing which is done by lowering a small amphora or pot down to the bottom of the sea in a shallow spot. An octopus likes to curl up in a cozy place and often slips into one of the amphorae. On his next round the fisherman pulls up a string of the pots and collects the octopi, which have been taken without a struggle or a big investment of time. It was not the season for octopus fishing, however, so thousands of the little amphorae were stacked up along the quays.

Late that afternoon we heard a commotion and looked across the harbor to see a parade with marching bands, fancy floats, decorated camels, uniformed students, caparisoned horses, and acrobats that wound past our view and disappeared toward town. "Nice of them to stage all this in our honor," said Margaret with a wink.

At dawn the next morning the whole world was one of pastels—light greenish water, the quiet blue of a pale sky, white clouds tinged with pink, the washed-out yellows on a fishing net hanging next to us, the soft colors of the fishing boats . . .

We shut up the yacht, walked to the inner harbor, and took a taxi to town, about three kilometers away. When we asked the driver about eating the lotus, we got a finger-waving lecture about the evils of drug use. When we inquired about the Odysseus festival, the driver brightened up.

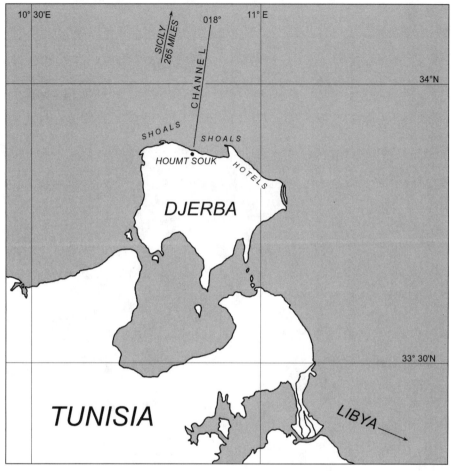

DJERBA IS A SMALL DESERT ISLAND JUST OFFSHORE FROM SOUTHERN TUNISIA.

"It's a parade and carnival we have every year to celebrate the great explorer. There are swimming competitions, a running marathon, camel races, and plenty of special food. Everyone has a good time. The school children love it, and it entertains the tourists."

I took a photograph of a festival banner while Margaret bought an *International Herald Tribune*. There were a lot of Berber women walking about, dressed in a single cloak-like garment that was draped over the head and down and around the body to the ankles. A sort of Mexican serape, only longer. The capes were all the same color (a light tan) and decorated with a few horizontal red-

July Festival, Houmt Souk, Djerba.

orange stripes, usually around the waist and bottom hem. The women wore a small straw hat on top of the cape. Some had a tuck or two of the dress across their face for religious reasons. Other women wore ordinary western dress. Most of the men had on short sleeve shirts and dark trousers.

We headed for the folkloric museum, walking on fine sand along the edge of the roads because we were in the desert. There were a few trees, and we noticed that the locals carefully arranged their walking routes to take advantage of the shade. Even the meager shade from the thin-leafed trees was better than no shade at all.

The museum was tiny and in an old domed thick-walled building, dark and cool inside. We saw a few old manuscripts in Arabic and half a dozen display cases with mannequins dressed in Berber wedding costumes and other ceremonial clothes. We looked at a display case with an explanation of local customs in French and Arabic and spent a while trying to work out the long sentences in French. We asked the curator about several meanings and received a lengthy explanation in French and some English. The light coming in through the entrance door illuminated the curator's face in a wonderful way as he spoke.

"The Berbers have a reputation for being sharp at commerce and are good businessmen," he said. "In the old days the Berbers only married within their own sect. Now, however, they will marry if their partner is a Muslim. In remote areas the Berbers are more conservative and stay within their own group."

We asked about the lotus. "There's a local legend that a stranger who comes to Djerba and stays is said to 'have taken the lotus,'" replied the curator. "In the old days you ate the leaves of a certain plant, but the sheep have nibbled it away, and the plant is gone.

"Part of the sentence in the display case says: '. . . envouter ceux qui ont goûté a son *Lotus*,'" said the curator. "This means to cast a spell on those who have tasted the lotus. In other words, our people are very welcoming. Visitors find Djerba a place of unique charm. Outsiders are made to feel at home."

"That fellow should be working for the tourist bureau," I said to Margaret when we were outside. "He's full of charm. A real salesman. He must be a Berber."

I wondered if sailors knew the lotus story before Homer's time? Could the yarn have circulated from port to port in the ancient world? Did Homer use it because it was a good story? I would like to think so, but the reality is that all the present-day talk about the lotus is after the fact of Odysseus, not before. Strangers who ask locals leading questions are always answered in ways that satisfy both the questioner and the native.

Tourism is big business in Djerba because of the sun, the beaches, and modest prices. The island has 76 hotels—rated at from one to five stars—with a bed capacity of 27,700. In 1995, there were 700,000 European visitors who came seeking the sun and beaches. If each visitor spent say $165 U.S. a day for a room, meals, taxis, drinks, souvenirs, entertainment, airfare, and stayed a week, Djerba had close to a billion-dollar tourist business!

We talked to Mme. Maherzia Gaddour in the fancy, new, air-conditioned government tourist bureau. "Yes, it is right," she said. "Christopher Columbus discovered America, and Odysseus discovered Djerba. Now the tourists have discovered Djerba."

"What about the lotus?" I asked. "What is this fruit? Can I buy it? Can I taste it? Will I be lulled into sweet dreams and indolence too?"

"Ah, that's the mystery of Djerba," she laughed, waving a paper under my nose. "The scientists have explained it in these pages, but I don't know about all their talk. Maybe it's the easiness of living here, the languor, the simplicity." She wrinkled her nose and smiled in a lovely way. "Perhaps everyone who is here has taken the lotus."

We talked about the lotus. Was it an herb? A drug? A narcotic? Or was it merely a state of mind brought about by the pleasantness of the country? Was it the lassitude engendered by the tropical temperatures that tended to keep strangers in Djerba? These last two sentences began to sound like public relations hype generated by tourist bureaus all over the world.

We left Mme. Gaddour and took a bus ride around Djerba. I was surprised how dry the island was. It really was the Sahara desert. The ground was bare and brown. Farmers had cut furrows here and there and heaped up the soil to try to retain moisture when it rained. There were date palms and olive trees, but they had to fight for moisture. The orchards seemed uneven and scraggly, except for one place we passed.

It was a long hot ride. The driver of our creaky old bus stopped often to take on or let off hotel staff going or coming from work. Almost everyone carried a bottle of water and took frequent drinks. On the ride back a young girl across from us passed out from heat prostration. She was about eleven years old and looked simply terrible. The man next to her asked me for my water bottle which I quickly passed across. Fortunately by this time our bus was just entering Houmt Souk. Two men carried the poor girl off the bus and whisked her away in the crowd.

Back on *Whisper* I studied Mme. Gaddour's scientific paper. To begin with, Homer doesn't give much of a description of the lotus. "It's the honeyed fruit of the plant," is his only comment.

Herodotus, writing in the fifth century B.C., said: "The lotus-fruit is about the size of the lentisk berry, and in sweetness resembles the date. The Lotus-eaters even succeed in obtaining from it a sort of wine."[23]

According to Pliny, in the first century A.D., it was the *cordia myxa*, a fruit that grows in clusters. Polybius, another writer of ancient times, stated that the lotus was a small, spiny tree with yellow flowers that produced a dark red edible fruit. "The taste approaches that of the fig and the date with an even more agreeable smell. From it one can prepare a delicious drink which has the taste of wine, but it doesn't keep for more than ten days." His description tallies somewhat with the wild jujube. This plant is close to the cultivated jujube—sometimes called the Chinese date—which today is found on Djerba where it forms thick clumps two or three meters high. The scientific paper droned on with speculation, rumor, and opinion.

I knew that whatever the fruit was in the real world, Homer called it the lotus. In his story he added to its taste and substance by making it addictive and causing forgetfulness and apathy. My big American Heritage dictionary defines lotus-eater as follows:

> **Greek Mythology:** One of a people described in the Odyssey who fed on the lotus and hence lived in a drugged, indolent state.

Let's remember that the Greeks who arrived in Djerba thirty-two centuries ago were exhausted and worn out from ten years of warfare. They had lost many of their comrades in combat and in the fighting with the Cicones in Ismarus. They had just survived a terrifying sea voyage to parts of the world unknown to them. Is it any wonder they liked the hospitable island people who welcomed them? No wonder the Greeks succumbed to the charms of the place. It was the fresh fruit, the roast lamb, a long sleep, and perhaps the companionship of women. Everything was new, different, and restful. These ordinary Greek seamen were suddenly on Mt. Olympus with the gods. Of course the men resisted Odysseus when they learned that their chief wanted to drag them off to sea again. Everyone who has suffered the horrors of a tempest on board a small vessel only a few feet from an angry ocean will understand the reluctance of a sailor to head out again.

SO FAR WE'VE VISITED TROY, Ismarus, Samothráki, Delos, Cape Malea, and Djerba. These are all real places that you can buy a ticket to. They're on maps, in atlases, in computer banks, and have coordinates of latitude and longitude. You can take photographs of them and buy souvenir postcards. Starting with this long trip to Africa, however, we've embarked on a part of the journey of Odysseus that may be real or it may be a grand tour of the imagination.

Many very bright and dedicated men and women have spent their lives tracing the places where Homer sent his most famous character. It's a question of reading the original, sifting the evidence, and deciding for yourself. Somewhere along this ancient track we make a 90° turn from the world of hard facts into the maybe arena of supposition and surmise. It seems clear to many people—but not all—that Homer wrote about places he'd never seen. Libraries didn't exist during his lifetime, but the great epic poet must have worked much like a modern author who digs into the minds and memories of others by interviews and association.[24]

As Homer composed his great story he learned about Africa and present-day Sicily and Italy by listening to travelers and foreign visitors. He gathered information from sailors and traders and explorers—anyone who had a story to tell about distant and marvelous places. If there was a bit of exaggeration now and then—well that was the way of the world. It was Homer's genius to people these distant worlds with characters that he knew perfectly and to describe them with golden sentences that even in translation have been admired for more than 2,000 years.

In chapter five I noted that a few people have interpreted Homer's clues to suggest that Odysseus might have gone into the Atlantic, to England, Iceland, or even America. These notions don't make any sense to a person who knows anything about small open boats, their limitations, and crew problems of olden times. Another idea that I mentioned earlier and that surfaces from time to time is that Homer

Fisherman and lateen sails, Houmt Souk.

and Odysseus were the same person and that *The Odyssey* is a travel account of Homer's voyages by Homer. This is possible, but doubtful. Certainly a poet as gifted as Homer who was on the scene would have mentioned obvious mountains, key islands, and such things as erupting volcanoes. A few writers have speculated that *The Odyssey* was a voyage confined to the local waters of Greece, but these scholars must talk their way clear of strong clues in the book and the weight of the opinion of the ancient world. A recent book by Tim Severin, for example, tells in detail how after failing to get permission to visit Libya he changed his southern itinerary to Crete. In his book Mr. Severin attempts to ignore the principal clue of nine days of voyaging described in book nine of *The Odyssey*. Djerba, of course, is not in Libya, but farther west in Tunisia where the author could have at least looked. Most people—both now and in the ancient world—believe that Djerba is the land of the lotus-eaters. In addition, Homer certainly had Sicily in mind for various parts of his story.

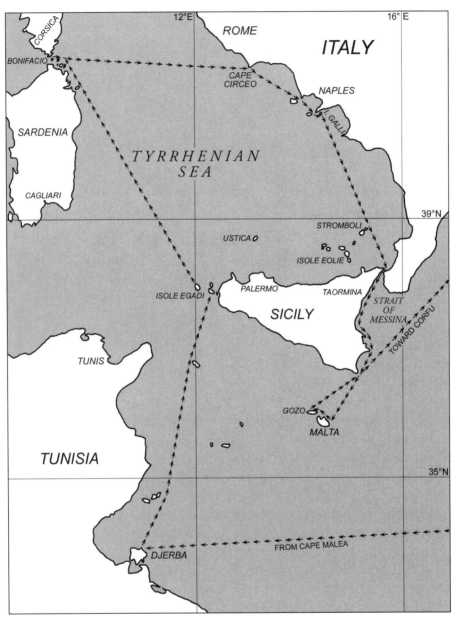

DJERBA TO THE TYRRHENIAN SEA.

POLYPHEMUS

O DYSSEUS KNEW HE WAS far south of Ithaca because of the desert heat of Djerba. He remembered the high temperatures in Egypt from an earlier trip. This was the same sort of heat, but the land in front of him was definitely not Egypt. On the long voyage to Djerba he had sailed south and west. His island home had to be in the opposite direction: to the north away from the desert; to the east toward the Ionian Sea.

Once away from land Odysseus may have set his course by angling slightly *toward* the morning sun on his right hand while it was close to the horizon. This would have established his course in relation to the wind and to the wave pattern which he could have maintained when the sun was high. Then in the late afternoon he could have checked that he was angling slightly *away* from the setting sun on his left hand. Odysseus— or a specialist among his crew—may well have used a sighting stick marked in angles or degrees or colors or notches to have worked out courses in relation to the sun. At night there were always a few stars to the north—Polaris, Kochab—and the constellation of Scorpio to the south.[25]

Thirty-two hundred years ago the angles were a little different, but the sailors had plenty of time to observe heavenly bodies and think about their steering courses (and verify their ideas while they were on land). Those whose thinking was clear and logical arrived at the next stop and in time sired and instructed new sailors; those whose ideas were confused simply disappeared. The sea always nurtures the survival of the bright.

On the first day—if the winds were southeast like the ones we experienced—the northward-bound warships passed east of the shoals that run eastward from the low island of Kerkennah off the coast of Tunisia. The next day the little fleet would have been at sea, west of Lampedusa island. On the third day his fleet was near the island of Pantelleria east of Cape Bon. The fourth night was dark with low clouds close overhead. There was heavy dew, and everything dripped with moisture. Fog swirled around the ships, and it was hard to keep them together. The wind dropped. The vessels sailed slowly, blindly. The men were apprehensive and afraid because the unknown is always spooky and uncertain. Night time is worse. And with clammy fog and around land, *night time is terrible.*

No one could see the land ahead until the long waves broke and scooped up the giant canoes and swept them up on a strange beach. The men saw white water swirling around them and heard the swell booming against the shore. And they'd never noticed a thing in the fog! Certainly one of the gods had looked after the fleet and saved their lives. The sailors quickly dragged their vessels to safety high on the beach, lowered the sails and the heavy masts, and slept.

When morning came, the warriors from Ithaca found themselves on the south side of a small island thickly set with brush and trees. The place was green and fertile and wholly uncultivated with no trace of man. Yet the island had soft moist meadows and rich soil where grain would thrive and vineyards flourish. In one place lay a harbor so protected that anchoring was scarcely necessary and where it would be easy to beach ships. At the head of the inlet, a spring bubbled with fresh water, and black poplars grew nearby. In 1200 B.C. the island was a first-class candidate for a Greek colony.

In coming north from Africa and crossing the Mediterranean the men had sailed 260 miles. They were on ancient

Aegusa or Goat island, known today as Favignana. Nearby are Marettimo and Lèvanzo, two other small islands. All three lie only a few miles from Sicily.

Everyone was hungry so when scouts spotted mountain goats the men grabbed their spears and bows and arrows. In a few hours they killed more than one hundred of the small animals. While the meat was roasting over fires the men took out a few jars of red wine they had brought from Ismarus. Soon everyone was eating and drinking and speculating about the smoke and fires they saw on the mainland to the east. They could even hear voices and the sounds of animals drifting across the water. The men were looking at the west coast of Sicily, also known as the land of the Cyclops. It was a place where giant, brutish, independent fellows lived in caves and paid little attention to their neighbors or the laws of ordinary men.

"My good friends," said Odysseus, "for the time being I want you to stay here, while I go in my own ship with my own crew to find out what kind of men are over there, and whether they are brutal and lawless savages or hospitable and god-fearing people."[26]

Everybody knows the story.

Fifty men rowed across to the mainland. After they landed, Odysseus took a dozen of his fellows, a sack of provisions and a goatskin of wine, and climbed to a big cave above the wooded shore. The cave was the home of a one-eyed giant named Polyphemus who raised sheep and goats and made cheese. Since he was away in the pastures with his flocks, the men were keen to steal the cheeses and drive the kids and lambs penned up at the entrance to the cave down to their ship and away to Goat island.

Odysseus said: "No. We'll wait."

Late in the day the giant returned and drove his nannies and ewes into the cave. His appearance terrified the sailors who retreated to the back of the cave. He closed the entrance with a huge boulder and began milking. Afterwards he lit a fire. As it flared up he spotted the strangers.

"Who are you?" he said.

Odysseus, never shy and always boastful, told a false story about a shipwreck. He boasted about the Trojan War, their travels, and asked for hospitality. Polyphemus called Odysseus a fool. Then he jumped up, seized two men, ripped them apart, and gobbled them up for his supper. Afterwards he lay down and was soon asleep. Odysseus thought of driving his sword into the giant's breast, but he realized that he and his men could never move the great stone that blocked the entrance.

The next morning Polyphemus woke up, milked his ewes, and ate two more men for breakfast. Then he opened the cave, let his animals out, replaced the huge entrance stone, and headed up to the pastures. Desperate and trapped inside the cave, Odysseus and his men cut six feet from the giant's staff, sharpened one end, and hid the makeshift spear in the cave. The plan was to wait until the giant was asleep. Then Odysseus and four of his fellows would ram the point into the eye of the Cyclops.

That evening the giant appeared with his flock. He opened the cave, led his charges inside, and closed the entrance with the great stone. After milking he devoured two more men.

Meanwhile Odysseus prepared a bowl of sweet wine and offered it to the giant. "Here's a treat for you, Polyphemus. Have some wine to wash down that meal of human flesh."

The Cyclops drank the bowl, liked it, and asked for a second bowl, which he also drank. "Tell me your name," he said, "so that I may make you a gift."

Odysseus talked while he prepared the third bowl. "My name is Nobody," he said. "Everybody calls me Nobody."

"Nobody?" roared the giant as he finished the wine. "I'll eat Nobody last. That's my gift to you!"

The wine made the giant's head swirl, and he soon fell to the floor, his face upwards. Odysseus and the four men quickly uncovered their spear, heated its point in the fire, and, with colossal force, thrust it into the eye of the giant, turning it round and round. It was gruesome work.

The giant awoke with a terrible scream. He jumped up

and managed to pull the pole from his ruined eye, which was streaming with blood. He could see nothing; he was blind. His shouts attracted his neighbors who rushed to the cave entrance.

"What's wrong with you, Polyphemus?" they said. "Is a robber driving off your sheep? Is somebody trying to kill you?"

"Oh my friends," he said, "it's Nobody's treachery, not violence, that's doing me to death."

"Well then," said his neighbors, "If nobody is assaulting you, you must be sick." And they went back to their caves.

The Cyclops, still in agony, groped about the cave. He pushed the great stone away from the entrance. Then he sat down at the mouth of the cave with his arms spread hoping to catch Odysseus and the six men who were still inside.

Odysseus, frantic now, was trying to think of a way to escape. He scooped up a handful of twigs, braided them into a kind of rope, and lashed three rams abreast. Then he tied a man under the middle ram with a ram on either side to shield him from the giant's hands. For himself, Odysseus took the big bellwether ram and clutched his thick coat from underneath with his hands and feet, hanging there face upward.

When dawn came, the rams began to leave the cave and head for the pastures. Polyphemus felt the back of each sheep as it went out, but never thought to put a hand underneath. All six companions of Odysseus slipped out of the cave. Finally the bellwether ram with Odysseus underneath trotted up to the entrance. The giant stopped him and stroked the animal.

"Dear old ram," he said, "why do you hang behind the others? Before, you were always first to reach the meadows. Do you feel for your master who's lost his eye? If I could only find that Nobody I'd smash his brains on the ground."

Odysseus, silent as death, hung on for his life. The ram trotted out of the cave. Odysseus freed himself from the animal and untied his men. Then they drove the sheep down to the ship where the waiting crew put them on board. They quickly pushed off and headed for Favignana.

Odysseus couldn't restrain himself. He shouted back to Polyphemus in the cave. "You brute! Who else but a monster would eat his own house guests?"

These taunts so enraged the Cyclops that he ripped the top from a great pointed rock and threw it at Odysseus. The rock landed just ahead of the ship, and the wash almost drove the vessel back to the beach. Odysseus grabbed a long pole and pushed off while he called to his crew to row like demons if they wanted to live.

Odysseus was still cocky. His men begged him to be still, but he shouted again: "Cyclops, if anyone ever asks you how you came by your blindness, tell him your eye was put out by Odysseus, Sacker of Cities, the son of Laertes, who lives in Ithaca."

The Cyclops screamed with anger and prayed to Poseidon that Odysseus might never reach Ithaca. Or if he did, that he would find a world of pain and anguish. The giant then picked up another huge stone and flung it at the ship. This time the rock fell just astern, and the resulting wave helped push the vessel toward Goat island. Once on the island the men beached the ship and unloaded the sheep, which were split among all the crews. The big ram was given to Odysseus who sacrificed the animal and burned slices of the sheep's thighs to Zeus of the Black Clouds. But Zeus took no notice.

The men—sore at heart at the loss of six of their comrades—feasted on the rich meat and drank more mellow wine. The next morning Odysseus ordered the men to sea.

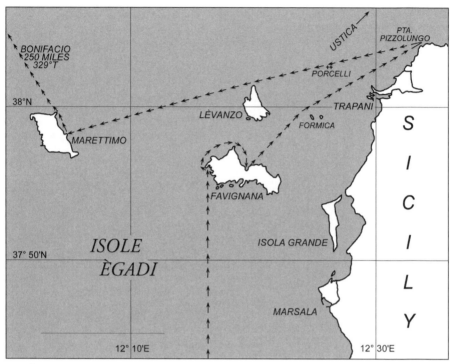

ÈGADI ISLANDS AND THE WEST COAST OF SICILY

FAVIGNANA
AND THE CAVE

AFTER LUNCH ON JULY 27TH we hoisted *Whisper's* sails in Houmt Souk, glided down the long entrance channel, and headed north across a shallow, turquoise-colored sea. Now we were aimed toward Italy and another phase of *The Odyssey.* The sun-baked islands of Greece were far away. The searing sands of Djerba lay behind us. Everything ahead would be new and different. Or would it?

The first night we sailed east of Iles Kerkennah off the Tunisian coast. A great mass of shallows and drying sandbanks runs east from this low island complex for twenty-five miles. Fortunately six powerful navigational lights mark the shoals. Though I knew our position and checked off each buoy as we rounded it, I was relieved to see the easternmost marker and to sail into deep water. On the second day we continued a little east of north with a southeast wind which faded away as the lights of the Italian island of Pantelleria hove into view. The yacht rocked gently on the quiet sea. Margaret and I took turns sleeping while we waited for the wind to return. North of Pantelleria we could see a steady line of big ships on the Gibraltar-Suez track.

As it grew light I noticed a yellow finch perched on one of the lifelines. It was tiny, only about three inches long, the smallest bird I'd ever seen. It must have come aboard in Tunisia. I hoped the bird would hang on until we sailed near Pantelleria because it was certainly too weak to make a long flight. By 0900 the southeast wind had come back. I fudged the course toward land. The little bird turned toward Pantelleria, unclasped its tiny claws from the lifelines, and flew off, making a jerky flight close to the water. Its future was doubtful, and it had no immigration papers for Italy, but I hoped the bird would make it.

"Goodbye, sweet bird," I called. "Good luck."

We pushed on toward Favignana, which emerged from haze and murk in the late afternoon. We had planned to anchor in Cala Grande near the western tip, but the swell from the southeast wind was rolling into the little bay. We went to the main port on the north side for the night.

The next morning the wind changed to the north. We sailed back to Cala Grande, anchored in clear water on a patch of sand in the small bay, and rowed ashore. The most obvious change since ancient times is the handsome forty-three-meter lighthouse on Punta Sottile at the western point of the bay, which is also the western extremity of the island. The only other structure around the shores is a small hotel in the cove at the southeastern end of the bay. You've already guessed the name: the Ulysses hotel.

Except for a small beach near the hotel, the shore was ringed by flint-hard, weathered, and cracked volcanic lava. Walking was hard in shoes and almost impossible for bare-footed swimmers. On the west-central part of the island a steep 302-meter ridge called Montagna Grossa crosses the island from north to south; an attractive eleventh-century Norman castle named Santa Caterina crowns the summit. These days it's an Italian military area, has an unmanned radar station, and is out of bounds.

Until a century ago the western slopes were forested with pines. Today the trees and topsoil are mostly gone, the island is no longer luxuriant, and the only goats on the island are domesticated. There used to be a little farming of wheat and barley, red and green grapes were grown for wine, and limestone blocks were quarried. Until recently the main business of the island was tuna. Every spring a mile-long net complex was erected in the sea to catch giant tuna on their annual migration from the western Mediterranean toward the Black Sea. The fish were canned in the island factory, owned by Ignazio Florio, which because of its low prices also canned tuna sent from as far away as Spain, Norway, and even Japan. [27]

Today the economics of canning are different. Favignana's once-prosperous cannery is closed, and the island lives on tourism. For the 2,900 local residents, Christmas comes in August when Italians from the mainland take their annual holiday. Then the main harbor is jammed with noisy ferries and hydrofoils. Nervous taxis and smoking buses wait along the quay. The hotels and pensions are packed, the restaurants crowded, the car-hire and scooter rental places sold out, and the ice cream parlors and discos full. Former farmers run tour boats, party fishing boats, dive boats, and gift shops; the locals are into summer home building and service jobs. With the trees gone and thousands of people on holiday during the summer, the natural springs have been sucked dry; tanker ships bring water from Trapani on Sicily. The once-pastoral island is as commercial as a drug store in Rome.

Since Homer's time the climate has become hotter and drier. During the summer the island's rough volcanic surface is always warm to the touch. Fortunately the island is surrounded by wonderfully clear water; swimmers and sun-worshipers love the sun-drenched island. The Italian government has declared much of the area a special marine national park.

But my business was with the ancient world. Did Odysseus stop at Favignana? Let's examine the evidence. Homer states that island X is uninhabited, modest-sized, wooded, has fertile land capable of being cultivated, and would be a good place for vineyards. He speaks of a safe harbor, and says that the island is near the mainland. He mentions fresh water and goats. Favignana has—or had—all these things. In addition, the ancient commentators thought that Favignana was a likely destination.

A weak point of the argument is that vessels running northward and entering Cala Grande or other anchorages on the south coast would have crunched into hard shoreline instead of a beach. Cala Grande has a beach, but it's hooked around to the right, hardly a place that twelve ships running northward would find in the dark. It's possible that long ago the hard shoreline had more topsoil and beaches or that an eruption from one of the nearby active volcanoes slightly altered the coastline.

Additionally, Cala Grande is sixteen miles from Punta Pizzolungo on Sicily, a likely site for the cave of Polyphemus.

The powerful light on Puna Sottile guards Cala Grande at the west end of Favignana.

The closest point from Favignana to the mainland is three miles to Isola Grande, an island immediately off the mainland (to which it was probably linked in the past). But Cala Grande is at the opposite, western end of Favignana, another five miles from the mainland. This means that if Cala Grande were the landing place, it would have been at least eight miles from the mainland, an impossible distance from which to hear the Cyclopes' voices and the bleating of the sheep and goats that Homer mentioned. But I'm slicing the banana with a razor blade. Maybe the landing place was at the *east* end of Favignana, which fits part of the account better and has a shore of diamond-hard lava no different from Cala Grande or elsewhere on this stony island. . . .

That night as evening fell, Margaret and I sat in the cockpit of *Whisper* when the great lighthouse above us turned on its magic lantern. I found it strange to be anchored fifty meters from a big lighthouse. At any moment there were four distinct rays as the giant white eye revolved. Every eight seconds two rays would turn 180° and stop. Then the other two would turn 180° and stop. I felt slightly hypnotized and couldn't keep from watching it. Even though the little bay of Cala Grande was wide open to winds and seas from the south, southwest, and west, the light gave me a marvelous sense of security and safety.

I wondered if Odysseus sat in his vessel in this same bay. There was no lighthouse then, of course, but perhaps he had the same sense of tranquility and well-being that I felt. Did he think about what was ahead? Did he despair or have hope? Did he worry about his six hundred men? Would he ever see Ithaca? Where would he stop next?

From Favignana, Margaret and I sailed toward the coast of Sicily. It was a slightly foggy morning, but as we made our way to the northeast the sun gradually burned off the mist. We could plainly see the buildings and harbor of Trapani. Our job was to find a certain prominent cave. Would we find a giant shepherd as well?

This was my first trip to western Sicily, and I half expected to see gangsters wearing felt hats blasting at each other with shotguns from behind hedges amidst a desolation of dust and poverty. But the Sicily I saw was nothing like the Hollywood version. Instead the sun glinted on the water and sprinkled a thousand diamonds on a coast that was a delicious green. Dramatic cliffs and steep hills plunged to the sea. In the distance I looked at stunning mountains and attractive red-roofed villages. Closer at hand I peered through my binoculars at a dozen vineyards with neat rows of leafy plants marching up the slopes.

At Punto Pizzolungo, five miles northeast of Trapani, I saw the cave: prominent, dark, unmistakable, a little above the

Looking west from the cave of Polyphemus, Pizzolungo Point,
near Trapani, Sicily.

coastal road above some houses. The cave was up a rocky slope
about a half-mile from shore, midway between the seaside ham-
lets of Pizzolungo and Bonagia. It was among the lower cliffs of
a mountainous face that extended inland. But how to visit the
cave? The coastal anchorage looked exposed and unsuitable.
We turned *Whisper* around, sailed back to the harbor at Trapani,
tied up the yacht, rented a small car, and drove northward along
the coastal road.

On the shore at Punto Pizzolungo we found a small settlement
of summer homes that ran inland—eastward—up the slope from
the sea and ended below the cliffs above. We drove to the end of
a steep and dusty lane (naturally called Polifemo street) and
parked the car. Then we crossed some old sheep fences and made
our way up the slope through a field of small eucalyptus trees.

Though only 1,500 feet or so above the houses, the cave seemed
isolated and separate, a great stone mouth that opened into the
base of a mountain. It was larger than I expected.

I stepped off a width of 90 feet and a depth of 55 feet, with two
slightly deeper places on the south side in back. The mouth of
the cave was about 25 feet high. Inside, the ceiling of the cave

was severely fire-blackened and showed long usage. There was a low drywall of loose flat rocks about 20 feet inside—parallel to the front of the cave—to keep sheep and goats from wandering away. The floor had many loose rocks ten or twelve inches across, presumably from the wall, which had partially tumbled down. The place was open and airy with a nice view of the sea. There was no smell of animals.

The trampled dirt floor of the cave was surprisingly clean except for plastic dishes and beer bottles left behind by recent picnickers. Several hundred small stalactites hung down two or three inches from the roof of the cave; some dripped slightly. No one knows what the entrance of the cave might have been like 3,000 years ago. Sections of the front may have collapsed during earthquakes or shepherds might have chipped it out. There had been a recent fire outside in front of the cave (probably set by someone tossing a cigarette from the cave) that blackened the field in front of the cave and killed a number of small trees and shrubs. The whole area reeked with the smell of burning.

I can't imagine closing this cave with a single huge boulder, but geologists say that cave mouths change severely over time and usually open wider because of earthquakes and avalanches.

In 1927, Bobbs-Merrill published a book by Richard Halliburton titled *The Glorious Adventure*. Halliburton exemplified the romantic school of travel writing and was widely criticized for his Sunday supplement writing style. Damn the truth. Give the readers a thrill. Let them experience vicarious excitement and emotion. Halliburton had a boyish enthusiasm for his subjects which shines through his writing and which his readers loved.

Halliburton visited the same cave where Margaret and I now sat. It had been raining hard. Halliburton and a friend who spoke Italian had walked out from Trapani and were soaked and miserable. When they finally entered the cave they found a fifteen-year-old barefoot Sicilian shepherd already installed with his flock of sheep. He was drying his blanket over a fire.

"Has this cave a name?" asked Halliburton through his friend.

"Ah, si, si. It is *La Grotta di Polifemo!*" said the shepherd. He added that it had that name because of a giant who had lived in the cave.

"Do you know the story about him?" asked Halliburton.

The young man shook his head.

It seemed tragic that the shepherd hadn't heard about his famous predecessor, so Halliburton and his friend told the wide-eyed boy the story of the brutal giant who ate men for breakfast and who almost gobbled up Odysseus as well. Halliburton described the blinding of the giant, the escape by holding themselves underneath the rams, and the anger of the giant when Odysseus taunted Polyphemus from his ship.

The shepherd peered around the cave with questioning, terror-struck eyes. Was Polyphemus liable to return?

Halliburton went on: "When the Cyclops learned that his enemies had escaped, he flew into such a rage that he broke off the top of a hill—perhaps it was the great rock that blocked the entrance—and hurled it at Odysseus. The huge missile missed the ship by inches and sank into the sea. Do you know about the little island out there called Formica?"

"Si, si, Signor," the shepherd replied with eager understanding. "Is that the rock that Polyphemus threw at them?"

"The very same rock. You can see how big Polyphemus must have been to throw a whole island that far."

The story finished and the hour late, the little group in the cave tucked themselves around the fire and went to sleep, perhaps wondering if the ghosts of the men that Polyphemus had eaten still drifted about in the shadows of the great cave.

Back aboard our yacht in Trapani we wondered if Homer had ever seen the cave at Pizzolungo. The odds are that he was never in this part of the world, but he could have heard about it from the crew of a Phoenician trading ship and incorporated it into his great tale. I'll never forget the place.

Birds often hitchhike on passing vessels. This perky yellow wagtail flew aboard
Whisper *near Trapani and hopped around the decks for a few hours. He took a
few sips of water but refused our bread crumbs and was last seen heading for the
island of Lèvanzo, flying at masthead height.*

THE WINDS
OF AEOLUS

FROM GOAT ISLAND Odysseus made his way to Aeolia, the home of Aeolus, lord of the winds. Aeolia was said to be a floating island, but sailors know that most small islands appear to move when seen from a ship, especially if a big swell is running. Homer doesn't tell us much about Aeolia except that it was an island ringed with a wall of bronze. Below the wall, steep cliffs fell away to the sea. A bronze wall in 1200 B. C. was, of course, a metallurgical impossibility. Presumably the wall around the island was made of wood or stone or some combination and covered with sheets of bronze or copper, which can be hammered very thin. Or perhaps in Homer's mind he saw the island when the golden rays of the setting sun fell on the cliffs. We don't know if the island of Aeolia was alone in the sea, part of a group of islands, near Sicily, or somewhere else. Aeolus appears in Homer's story as the ruler or king of the island. Later he's described as a minor god.

In any case Aeolus and his wife lived in a spacious palace in a kind of city-state. They had six sons and six daughters, and these fourteen happy islanders had a contented life with plenty of luxuries. Every day the smell of roasting meat and other delights drifted through the palace along with the pleasant sounds of a flute. The family was a little unusual because the six sons were married to the six daughters, a situation generally frowned upon because of problems with offspring. Nevertheless, incest didn't bother the ancient Egyptians, and apparently didn't concern Aeolus.

"After we arrived on the island, Aeolus was my kind host for an entire month," said Odysseus. "He was keen for news, so I gave him a full account of our expedition to Troy and our start for home."

When the fleet was ready to sail, Odysseus asked Aeolus for directions and assistance. Aeolus agreed to help and gave Odysseus a stout bag made of ox hide in which he imprisoned all the blustery winds. Aeolus went aboard Odysseus's ship, personally stowed the bag in the hold, and bound it with silver wire to prevent any leaks. Since he was the steward of the winds and could make them strong or weak at will, he sent a fresh west wind as the fleet of twelve headed out to sea.

The long slim warships rushed off and were soon out of sight. They hurried along for nine days and nights and made good progress. Odysseus kept his hand on the mainsheet of his vessel most of the time and on the tenth day actually saw Ithaca and people on shore. Relieved to have finally arrived home but exhausted from his long watches, he fell asleep.

With the captain out of the way, the crew began to whisper among themselves. The men were well aware of the leather bag that Aeolus had brought on board. They were certain that it contained a fortune in gold and silver and that it all belonged to Odysseus.

"Why should *he* receive such gifts when we, who have gone through as much as he has, get nothing?" they cried to one another.

The more the men talked, the bolder they became. Finally they undid the silver wire on the leather bag so they could see the treasure. As soon as the bag was opened, the winds rushed out. A storm with contrary winds blasted down on them, and all the ships were carried back out to sea. When Odysseus felt the boat roll, he awoke and saw Ithaca disappearing astern. He was so distraught that he considered jumping overboard and drowning himself. But he hung on. The storm from the east drove the ships all the way back to Aeolia.

When the vessels arrived, Odysseus and two men went to the palace. Aeolus and his family were amazed to see Odysseus.

"What happened?" they cried. "We gave you everything you needed to get home."

Odysseus explained that the ships had sailed within sighting distance of Ithaca. But he was so tired from handling the mainsheet that he nodded off. While he was asleep his crew had opened the leather bag and the winds escaped. He apologized.

"Will you help us again?" he pleaded.

Aeolus jumped to his feet: "Go quickly from this island!" ordered the king, his face flushed with anger. "The world has no greater sinner than you. I cannot help any man who is despised by the blessed gods. Go! Your presence here is proof of their hatred."

Abruptly dismissed by Aeolus and humiliated, Odysseus left the palace and walked slowly back to his ships.

EVERYONE KNOWS THIS SIMPLE, timeless story. The question is where did it take place? Was this tale an invention of Homer? Or the recounting of a fable handed down the centuries? The account is sparse and makes the reader thirst for more information. First of all we have a small island surrounded with a bronze wall that somehow supports a king and his large and happy family. There's no mention of other people or crops or livestock or ships or anything else. Homer speaks of roasted meats so we know there must have been cattle or sheep or goats, which in turn suggests meadows and grazing. There's talk of soft-piled rugs, which means spinning and weaving and probably slaves to do this work for the large royal family. Likewise, the elaborate meals for many suggest a staff of cooks and serving people.

In 1897 the English writer Samuel Butler made a long and complicated argument for locating Aeolia on the island of Ustica. This small, isolated island is sixty-three miles northeast of Favignana, an easy distance for the ships to travel, and a logical direction for Odysseus to have taken his fleet. But Ustica is thirty-two miles offshore from the *north* side of Sicily. The west wind mentioned by Homer would have blown him toward the west coast of Italy. He could then have gone south past Scylla and Charybdis, through the Strait of Messina, south of Italy, and on to Ithaca, but this route comes later in the story. In the ancient world, Scylla and Charybdis were considered major hazards and certainly would have been mentioned if the fleet had passed them.

Homer says specifically that Aeolus sent a *west* wind to blow Odysseus back to Ithaca. This means that if modern Ustica is the island of Aeolia, the ships of Odysseus would have had to weather the *west* end of Sicily, not an easy task for the clumsy vessels of long ago. Of course the men could have *rowed* around the west end of Sicily, but in the face of a strong wind from the west? Not likely. Could they have sailed? Not with their low-aspect square rigs and in ships without keels. There was no way they could have fetched the west coast of Sicily even if Aeolus's wind had veered to the northwest.

If Ustica is doubtful, where else? In the ancient world, Aeolia was often considered to be one of the seven Eolie islands, which are off the northeast corner of Sicily. Stromboli—with its simmering live volcano—was usually the first choice. But if we pick one of these islands the argument of using the west wind becomes even more difficult because Stromboli is 142 miles from the west coast of Sicily, a long and impossible slog to windward.

During our months in Italian waters Margaret and I read all the clues, studied the charts, and sailed entirely around Sicily. We stopped at isolated Ustica and all seven of the tiny Eolie islands (Alicudi, Filicudi, Salina, Lipari, Vulcano, Panarea, and Stromboli).

My choice for Aeolia is Marettimo, the westernmost island in the Ègadi group at the west end of Sicily. Marettimo is eighteen miles west of Sicily and ten miles west of Favignana. Certainly any arguments for selecting Ustica apply equally to Marettimo. But my main reason for deciding on Marettimo for the home of Aeolus is that it fits the west wind criterion so much better than Ustica or Stromboli. From Marettimo, Odysseus would have had an almost clear run along the south coast of Sicily; then to the Ionian Sea and Ithaca.[28]

Samuel Butler appears to argue against his choice of Ustica over Marettimo:

While sailing west into the setting sun, Marettimo seemed more like a dream.

> As regards 'the wall of bronze' which the writer of the *Odyssey*
> tells us ran round the island of Aeolus, it is hard to say whether it
> was purely fiction or no. We may be sure that it was no more
> made of bronze than Aeolus was king of the winds, but all round
> the island of Marettimo, wherever the cliffs do not protect it
> naturally, there existed a wall of long pre-Odyssean construc-
> tion, traces of which were shown me by Sigr. Tedesco and Pro-
> fessor Spadare, without whose assistance I should not have
> observed them. . . . no traces of any such wall exist so far as I
> know on Ustica, nor yet on the islands of Favignana or Levanzo.[29]

Marettimo is four miles long and a mile-and-a-quarter wide
with the main dimension of the island running almost north and
south. The island is split by a high ridge along the middle, from
Mt. Falcone (686 m.) in the north to Punta Lisandro (482 m.) in
the south. The island is steep-to and mountainous and has no
safe harbors, but depending on the wind and swell, there are a
few anchorages. The Mediterranean is narrow here—it's only sev-
enty-five miles to Cape Bon in Africa—and during the Napole-
onic wars (1803–15) the British fleet set up a lookout station on
the northeast point to watch for French warships.

Marettimo is the most verdant of the Ègadi group by far. The forest service maintains a network of public footpaths to such places as a Bourbon castle, the lighthouse near Punta Libeccio, ancient Roman houses, and a 12th-century Norman church. With luck you're liable to see mountain goats and wild boars. From high points on the island the views are superb in all directions, and the mood of the place is one of incredible blueness.

The sole village on Marettimo (900 people) is on the east slope of the island where a point of land sticks out. There are marginal anchorages on each side of the point. The ferries use the south bay. We went to the north, launched the dinghy, put out a second anchor, and rowed ashore. Again we were in a busy community because of the summer season, but the island was much less crowded than noisy Favignana.

As we walked around, two men in rough clothing in their forties came up to us and began talking in mile-a-minute Italian. They assumed we were Italians on vacation and tried to sell us a rowing trip to a nearby beach, which they claimed was spectacular.

"Only 30,000 lire [$19]," they said. We were assured that we'd be safe with them. . . . How wonderful it would be for us to be on the sea for an hour or two. . . . "Il mare è bello e le grotte sono grandi."

Margaret and I both smiled. Little did they know that we'd spent our lives sailing all over the world, and for the past couple of years had been crisscrossing the Mediterranean . . .

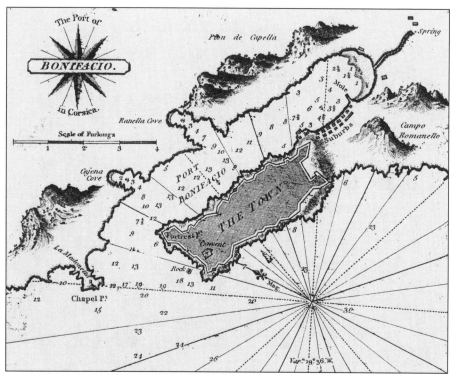

A *drawing of Bonifacio from the British Pilot of 1804. At that time the population of the fortified village up on the cliff was about the same as today, 2,433.
Note that this plan is done in* furlongs. *(One furlong is 660 feet or 1/8 of a
land mile.)*

13

THE
LAESTRYGONIANS

G ET OUT! Get out! Get away from my island," ordered King Aeolus.

Odysseus & Co. had no choice but to obey. The
men from Ithaca rowed away silently, humiliated, their heads
bowed. Odysseus was furious at his crew for opening the
bag of winds, but anger wouldn't restore the prized west wind
which was gone, finished, wasted. . . .

Think of it! He had actually seen the hills and shores of
Ithaca! His homeland! He had been close to his wife and
son. Then the cursed gale from the wrong direction had
come and blown the ships away. Now Ithaca was only a
memory, and he was far, far to the west. If only he hadn't
fallen asleep.

There was no wind, so the men pulled hard at their oars.
Soon Aeolia was lost in the distant mists. When the first set
of rowers slumped with weariness, others took over, and the
first day became the second. The men drank water from the
clay jars and ate rations of olives and dried fish. They shouted
encouragement from one ship to the next. The third day
turned into the fourth. The rowers ate onions, shellfish, and
cheese. The men at the steering oars were careful to keep
the fleet together and not allow anyone to fall behind or pull
ahead. Some of the warriors slept while others rowed, and
on and on they cruised. Finally on the seventh day the little

fleet came to Telepylus, the stronghold of the Laestrygonians.

The sailors saw a long line of high, vertical cliffs ahead. As they steered toward the unbroken wall that rose from the sea, one of the men spied a crack between two of the headlands. The narrow opening led to a marvelous harbor, a sheltered place with total protection from wind and swell. The captains of eleven of the ships headed in and tied up close together.

"I didn't follow them," said Odysseus. "Instead I brought my ship to rest outside the cove and tied her to a rock at the end of the point. Then I climbed the headland to get a view from the top."

In the distance Odysseus saw a wisp of smoke. He sent three men to investigate. The scouts found a wagon track and a girl drawing water from a spring. She was the daughter of Antiphates, chief of the Laestrygonians. The scouts tried to question the girl about the people, but she sent them to the house of her father. There they met the wife of Antiphates, a huge woman whose appearance terrified them. The woman summoned her husband, who immediately grabbed one of the scouts, tore him apart, and ate him on the spot.

The other two men fled back to the ship. Meanwhile Antiphates sounded a general alarm, and hundreds of huge Laestrygonians hurried to the edge of the cliffs above the fleet. The giants picked up boulders and began to bombard the ships below. The rocks smashed the ships and killed many of the men outright. The screams of the others were horrible. The giants then flung spears attached to lines, hooked the men, pulled them up like twitching fish, and took them away for their loathsome meals.

When Odysseus saw this ghastly scene inside the harbor he whipped out his sword and cut the mooring lines between his ship and the shore. Meanwhile he shouted to his crew to jump on board and row for their lives. The men obeyed instantly and the ship shot out to sea. But the other eleven ships were lost and all the men killed. From 668 men and twelve fighting ships after Troy, Odysseus was down to a single vessel and fifty men. It had been a slaughter.

• • •

SOME OF HOMER'S LOCATIONS are easy to find. Others are not. But most ancient and modern scholars (not all) agree on the whereabouts of Circe's island, the Siren Rocks, and Scylla and Charybdis. The whereabouts of Calypso's cave is more questionable. The Land of the Laestrygonians was long thought to be mythical. Yet thirty-five years ago the sailor-historian Ernle Bradford accidentally discovered that the harbor of Bonifacio at the southern extremity of Corsica fitted all the clues. Bonifacio is one of the few places in the Mediterranean with complete shelter behind high cliffs; the anchorage mirrors Homer's description exactly:

> A harbor ringed on all sides by precipitous cliffs, with a narrow entrance channel between two bold headlands.

The buff-colored limestone bluffs that front this part of Corsica are unique in the Mediterranean. The only similar—and not nearly as spectacular—place that I know of is Pórto Koufó on the Khalkidhikí peninsula in the northwestern Aegean sea in Greece. Bonifacio also fits in well with the general story and with Favignana and Marettimo on the west coast of Sicily and Cape Circeo on the west coast of Italy.[30]

We decided to have a look for ourselves and sailed northwest from the island of Marettimo toward Corsica on the afternoon of August 20th. The distance is 248 miles. We started out with a fresh wind from the north-northwest, but it was only an island breeze and died two hours later. We were becalmed all night, so we hung up a bright light and had a good sleep on a deserted ocean.

The next morning while Margaret was cooking pancakes, a northbound Spanish container ship came by and gave us a friendly toot on her whistle. Everybody waved. By noon we had the spinnaker up, but again the wind failed. At this rate the summer would be gone before we saw Corsica. We poked along at a few knots while cumulonimbus clouds piled up in the west. At midnight, forked lightning flashed in every direction, and we heard the rumble of thunder. Vertical bolts of lightning—sometimes single, sometimes double, all slightly reddish in color—knifed through the sky. Starting in the southeast, the wind clocked right around in a circle. A few sprinkles of rain cooled the air.

Limestone cliffs, southern Corsica.

We knew there'd be a change in the weather. Sure enough, an hour later we had a three-meter swell. By 0200 our sails rattled with twenty-four knots of wind from the northwest. A mistral, the dry cold wind from France, had arrived. I soon had two reefs in the mainsail, and we were bashing along toward Corsica, either on the northerly tack or the westerly. We'd come a long way north from southern Tunisia, and even though it was summer, at night the weather was sometimes cool enough for a sweater or jacket. Maybe we were getting soft.

Because of the swell, short seas, and an apparent wind of twenty-eight knots we were making only four knots with a miserable motion, but we hammered onward. We kept careful watches because of north-south shipping and big ferries crossing between the Italian mainland and Sardinia. By dusk the next day we could see a dim row of mountains among the distant clouds to the west. The following morning we were in smooth water and threading the coastal islands near La Maddalena island at the northeast corner of Sardinia. We anchored for the night.

When I looked out the next morning the mistral was still alive, but less strong. We got underway and cleared the small islands. Ahead we could see the south end of Corsica and a line of whitish cliffs. As we crossed the strait and neared the land we saw that erosion and natural causes had scarred the limestone cliffs with great fissures and cracks. Here and there they had tumbled into the ocean, leaving white pinnacles in a sea of intense blue. I thought the south coast of Corsica might be chockablock with high-rise apartments and hotels, but the area is still wild and beautiful and unspoiled. It's a unique coast in the Mediterranean.

We made a couple of tacks to the west near the land and took turns examining the cliffs with the binoculars. The high vertical cliffs were prominent, but there was no opening. The chart must be wrong! But charts are seldom wrong; it's the sailors who use them. We maneuvered closer. Still we could see no opening. We both jumped when we heard a ship's horn behind us. It was a ferry from Sardinia. She slipped past us and headed for the cliffs. Then she turned a little and disappeared. We followed and presto! We saw the entrance and then the lighthouse—painted red— which had been quite invisible to us. The high cliffs camouflaged the opening perfectly.

Once inside we marveled at the narrow channel with deep water. It has a width of only 185 meters and appeared to go nowhere. Yet the pilot book said that in the old days, large ships were warped in. Sure enough we saw great bollards spaced along the vertical walls just above the water. We followed the channel,

The entrance to Bonifacio.

Aerial view of Bonifacio.

turned 45° to starboard, and passed a tiny bay on the left (with half a dozen moored yachts). Ahead we saw tall buildings and a mass of docks and fishing boats and yachts. A vessel in Bonifacio was certainly protected from the sea. Yet anyone below and on the water was vulnerable to rocks pushed over the edge from the cliffs above. I looked up, wondering if someone was about to drop boulders on us. People were up above and walking along the edge of the cliffs, but they were tourists and armed only with cameras.

Someone, somehow, told Homer about this singular place and he made it part of his story.

In an hour we were tied up and ashore in a seaside cafe, having a coffee with a happy throng of summer people. The French flags snapped in the brisk wind from the mistral. The sun was warm and bright, the sky bright blue, and everyone bubbled with laughter and vitality. Nearby we heard a crowd of young French people singing at the tops of their voices. It was a lovely afternoon.

Both the harbor and the venerable village on the cliffs above had smart restaurants and shops. Everything was neat and trim, and the walkways to the village had elegant stone steps. We even managed to fill *Whisper's* tanks with sparkling fresh water, something impossible in much of Sicily and Greece. In all, our arrival in Bonifacio was delightful. There were no man-eating giants. No rocks thrown down from the cliffs. Only smiles and waving people.

Our sail from Marettimo had been slow and poky and included a lot of tacking. Certainly Odysseus could have beaten us with his oars. But only if he'd gone northward in the immediate shadow of the sheltered east coast of Sardinia. Out in the ocean his open boats and crude rigs would have failed.

Did Homer ever see the harbor of Bonifacio? Did he sail into the place on a lazy summer afternoon with fluffy clouds billowing into an azure sky above the shimmering cliffs? Did he pass from a spray-drenched sea into the millpond behind the twin

Bonifacio harbor.

headlands at the entrance? The romantics would like to say yes and erect a granite monument. The reality, however, is that Homer, living on an island in the eastern Aegean, probably heard about the place from a passing sailor who traded his recollections for a bowl or two of wine.

Much of the background and language of The Odyssey appears to be based on descriptions and practical details from sailors' manuals. The ancients called such nuts-and-bolts material periploi, kataploi, and stadiasmoi. In later years, sailors' accounts were known as portulans, mirrors, torches, or track charts. Today a sailor heading for a strange coast reads a pilot or browses through sailing directions to find out about local winds, dangerous rocks, approach channels, harbors, whether the natives are friendly, and so on. In Homer's world this information must have been rudimentary and perhaps passed along by word of mouth.[31]

One thing I know as a sailor is that you always question those who have gone before you. What were the winds like? The storms? The best season for navigation? The harbors? The anchorages? The fishing? The people? What things do they want? (On an early Pacific trip I remember being told to take cigarettes, .22 shells, jars of mayonnaise, and lots of stainless steel fishhooks.)

The information from sailing directions helps sailors make easier and more efficient (translation: profitable) voyages for their own ship or company. In the early days the sailing directions were often kept secret or private. Sometimes sailors even passed out false or misleading information to discourage competition. The Dutch went to scandalous lengths to discourage foreign sailors from the Far East spice trade as recently as 300 years ago. After the invention of printing, a few national governments wrote and distributed sailing instructions to improve general trade and transport. But presumably at the time of the Trojan War there was no writing and hence no pilot books. In Homer's time, 450 years later, there was some crude writing, but how much, who did it, what a scribe wrote on, and the details of distribution and comprehension are unknown.

Associated with this is the whole arena of languages: who spoke what? How did people communicate? It's doubtful that men from Sicily and Ithaca and Troy spoke the same tongue. I presume that Homer had Odysseus and Polyphemus, for example, speak Greek—his language—to one another because Homer's first audience was Greek. A storyteller must communicate to his audience.

The late Victor Bérard, a man passionately sympathetic to Homer and who wrote a whole shelf of books on the subject, had an even more intriguing notion. We know that the Trojan War took place about 1200 B.C. We believe that Homer composed his story about the conflict in 750 B.C. or so, some 450 years later. Yet it wasn't until 750 B.C. and afterwards that at least seventeen cities on what is now the south Italian coast were settled by the Greeks. Could these Greek colonists have taken storytellers (who knew Homer's stories) with them and sought the locations mentioned in the text and named them accordingly?[32]

Could the place we know today as Circe's island, for example, have been named *after* Homer had somehow passed on *The Odyssey*? Until 750 B.C. there was no writing. Even then who knows how widespread it was? I can guess at the snide comments of the elders: ("It's a fad and simply won't last.").

I don't think that Bérard's idea has much merit because it comes after the fact, not before. Nevertheless I salute his scholarship. It makes me think of the Greeks I met in the bookstore in Alexandroúpolis who said: "In our search for the truth we must overlook nothing."

Could Bonifacio have been home to a race of lawless giants? I close my eyes and try to think of the harbor in 1250 B.C. Then there would have been no tall buildings, no extensive docks, no patrolling gendarmes, no buses, no street lights, no gasoline station, no line of restaurants, no parking lots, no banks, no cash machines. I would have seen small houses, irregular fields of grain and grapes and vegetables, sheep and goats and cattle. . . . Would the community have been a peaceful and dreamy land of simplicity and basic values? Things like who had the prettiest wife and the nicest hut? Who was the best hunter? Or were the men scrabbling for position and power and planning the next war? I'd like to say it was peaceful and dreamy and idyllic, but if the real world of the ancient Greeks was like Homer's books I would have to say that it was man vs. man and god help the weak and timid.

Near the summit of Mt. Circeo, 44 miles southeast of Rome.

CIRCE

AFTER ODYSSEUS LEFT CORSICA, he traveled east toward the Italian mainland. Instead of twelve splendid vessels, however, there was now only one, a pathetic remnant of the proud fleet that had sailed from Ithaca almost twenty years earlier. The men who were left were tired and weary. Their hair was streaked with gray, and they moved slowly and with resignation. Their jokes were fewer and more cynical. Sometimes the survivors glanced at the men around them and wondered who would be the next to go?

How many were still alive? I worked out in chapter six that 742 men had set off from Troy. After the battle in Thrace there were 616. The Cyclops took six, which left 610 or about 51 men for each of the twelve ships. Following the deluge of rocks by the Laestrygonians that destroyed eleven ships and the orgy of cannibalism that consumed their crews, only a single ship remained. It was the one captained by Odysseus, with 44 men, a ragtag remnant of the fleet. The battle at Ismarus and the fighting with the Cicones must have seemed heaven on earth compared to what had happened since. . . .

The solitary ship traveled east toward the morning sun. The men were thankful to be alive, but they felt sad and miserable when they thought of their dead comrades. They missed traveling with the other vessels and the spirit of friendly rivalry when they rowed and sailed. Yet such is the buoyancy of the human spirit that after a few days they began to recover a little.

According to legend and tradition, Odysseus landed on the west coast of Italy on a south-facing peninsula thirteen miles north of 41° north latitude—halfway between present-day Rome and Naples. At the end of the peninsula is a large, mountainous island whose ancient name was Aeaea but today is called Circeo. Actually Circeo isn't an island at all, but looks exactly like one because low, marshy land lies to the north and east and from the sea isn't visible at all.

When they arrived, everyone was exhausted from rowing. The men eased the ship into the harbor, made camp, and spent two days sleeping and trying to shake off the deaths of their comrades. On the third day Odysseus, always curious and full of restless energy, climbed a nearby high point to look around. He saw that they were on an island. Nearer at hand he noticed a plume of smoke rising from the oak forest and decided to send out a scouting party. While he was returning to camp, an immense stag with a great rack of antlers ran in front of him. Odysseus killed him with his bronze spear and staggered back to the harbor with the carcass.

"Listen to me, boys," he said flinging the animal down. "We still may be grieving, but we're not finished yet. Let's have something to eat."

The men roasted the meat, drank the usual mellow wine, and began to feel better. The next morning Odysseus told everyone about his reconnaissance. But when he mentioned the plume of smoke the men—anticipating more trouble—began to weep.

In spite of resistance Odysseus split his forty-six-man party into two groups. He took one, and put Eurylochus, his lieutenant, in charge of the other. The two leaders shook lots, and Eurylochus, who lost the toss, set off. After a time the scouting party arrived at Circe's palace, an elegant structure on a cleared hill. Surprisingly tame wolves and lions roamed the grounds.

Circe, the sorceress with the luxuriant tresses, was inside her palace, singing sweetly as she wove a gorgeous fabric on her loom. When the scouting party called, she came out and invited the men inside. Everyone went except Eurylochus who suspected foul play. Once in the palace Circe prepared refreshments of cheese, barley, and honey mixed with wine. Unknown to the others she also stirred in magic drugs. When they finished their bowls, Circe touched each man with her wand. In a twinkling they were turned into pigs, and she drove the squealing animals to a sty.

Eurylochus, watching from outside, hurried back to the ship and reported what he saw. Odysseus quickly armed himself and set off for the palace. As he was going through the woods the god Hermes appeared, warned him about Circe, and gave him a special drug to neutralize her potions. In addition Hermes told Odysseus that when Circe touched him with her wand he should draw his sword and threaten to run her through. "She'll invite you to her bed," said Hermes. "You should accept. But make her swear by the gods that she'll not harm you or your men."

When Odysseus reached the palace, he called out. Sure enough, Circe invited him inside. She mixed her usual potion in a golden bowl and gave it to her guest to drink. Then she tapped Odysseus with her wand. "Get thee to the sty," she cried. "Wallow there with all your friends!"

Odysseus drew his sword and rushed at Circe as if he were going to kill her. She screamed, ran up and fell at his knees, and begged him not to kill her.

"Who are you?" she cried. "How can you drink my herbs and not be hexed? No man has ever resisted my potions. There's only one answer: You must be Odysseus. One of the gods told me that you'd stop here on your way back from Troy. Now put your sword away, and come with me to my bed where in love and sleep we can learn to trust each other."

Before Odysseus agreed to stay with Circe he made her swear to refrain from further mischief and to give his men their freedom. Circe swore a solemn oath and changed the pigs back to humans. Afterwards she sent Odysseus to his ship where the rest of the crew was waiting and had them haul the vessel ashore and store all the gear in nearby caves.

When Odysseus and the men returned to the palace and met their comrades, lately returned from being pigs, everyone burst into tears. Circe and her winsome maids bathed and clothed the entire party, gave them meat and wine, and told them to rest and be merry.

"Royal son of Laertes," said Circe to Odysseus. "I want you and your comrades to stay here with me until you regain your strength and spirits." Her enticements won the hearts of the Greek warriors, and little by little the days became weeks which turned into months. This pleasant interlude lasted for a year. Finally, however, the men became impatient.

"Master, it's time to return to Ithaca," they implored.

Odysseus asked Circe to let him go home as she had once promised. The goddess reluctantly agreed, but first sent him and his ship on a journey to the Land of the Dead, an imaginary place in the darkness of the Underground World where Odysseus spoke with the souls of the departed. He talked with the ghost of his mother, the murdered Agamemnon, and dozens of others. The Shade—the disembodied spirit—of each person reviewed the agonies and successes of his life on earth. Tiresias, the high priest of the Underworld, warned Odysseus not to molest the sacred cattle of the sun god when he stopped at Thrinacia island on his way back to Ithaca. Finally Odysseus ended his visit to the Land of the Shades. He commanded his rowers to pull again, and they swept into the rising daylight of a golden dawn and once again headed for Circe's island.

When he and his shipmates returned, Circe was ready with food and wine and instructions for sailing south. Again Odysseus heard the warning: "Do not molest the cattle of the sun god."

MARGARET AND I LEFT BONIFACIO aboard *Whisper* on September 6th at 0900 and sailed eastward past the small islands between Corsica and Sardinia. The upper village at Bonifacio disappeared in a few minutes, but we could see the splendid white cliffs on the south coast of Corsica for a long time. The tail end of a mistral whistled softly in our rigging, and with a fair wind *Whisper* rushed through the water. She was slightly out of control, so we rolled up the jib and tied one reef in the mainsail. Half an hour later we put in a second reef. The wind increased to thirty-four knots so we shortened the mainsail still again. Even with this tiny sail we skimmed along at 6.5 to 7.5 knots. Since we were in the lee of Corsica the sea was smooth; a significant swell didn't appear until we were out twenty miles.

Our goal was Cape Circeo on the Italian mainland, a distance of 178 miles. Circe's island has been the unanimous choice of practically all the ancient and modern scholars of Homer. But did Odysseus really come this way? Or were we chasing another will-o'-the-wisp? Bonifacio, which we had just left, fitted all the clues perfectly. Now we were on course for the next stop. What would we find?

Unlike sailing trips in the Southern ocean where in a single day we'd come across albatrosses, petrels, prions, fulmars, skuas, and terns we saw few pelagic birds in the Mediterranean. This was a pity because we're great bird fanciers. During the afternoon Margaret called me on deck.

"Look at those big birds circling around," she said. "What are they?"

I saw a short, chunky body (18–21") that was dark brown on top and white underneath. The wings were almost four feet long and also dark brown on top and white underneath. There was a short, dark, wide tail and a large hooked bill with the nostril tube along the top. The flight pattern was invariably several deep wing beats followed by a long, low glide.

I sat in the cockpit with the binoculars and Peter Harrison's 1983 *Seabirds* book across my knees and identified these thin-winged fliers as Cory's shearwaters. I wondered if the ancestors of these graceful birds had looked down at the black warship of Odysseus from their aerial world.

The wind continued from the west, but gradually eased. We countered with more mainsail area and poled out a headsail. During the night we watched big ferries and hydrofoils running between Sardinia and the Italian mainland as well as giant cruise ships that seemed more like luminous floating cities with their thousands of festive lights. Certainly we were an insignificant pinprick with our single masthead light and its 25-watt bulb.

By dawn the wind was almost gone, and we wished that our

A view from aloft of Whisper *sailing east across the Tyrrhenian Sea. The line that appears to be in the water to the left is the starboard running backstay. The standing backstay (of wire) is not visible. The loose line to the right goes to a fishing lure. The yacht is under the control of the Monitor steering vane while Margaret sits in the cockpit and keeps an eye on the course and watches out for shipping traffic.*

were twice as high. At noon a weather front passed us and brought 22 knots from the east. We tied the reefs back in. That evening the wind fell to nothing and later started up from the north. The fluky winds of the Mediterranean were certainly chasing us. By then, however, we'd spotted Cape Circeo in the distance. It was high, dark, distinct, and—sure enough—looked exactly like an island.

We still had twenty-seven miles to go. There was no way we could make the island before dark. We learned long ago never to enter strange ports after dark, and we knew that San Felice—the harbor we were heading for—was especially hazardous because of an encroaching sand bar. We reduced sail and poked along until morning, taking three-hour turns watching for ships and the five-second flashing light on the south face of the cape.

The next morning we followed a ferry from the island of Ponza into San Felice. It was a pretty area with large leafy trees and big houses on the steep slopes above the port. The water was calm, and the early sun made Circe's island golden and beautiful. I was glad we hadn't tried a night entry because the ferry circled north to miss the sand bar that blocked all but a narrow slot a stranger would never have found. We nosed in gently to a small port jammed to bursting. I'd never seen a harbor so crowded.

All the boats were moored in a way that was new to me. Instead of yachts being tied alongside a dock, each vessel was placed at right angles to the dock, with the bow facing out and the stern secured to the dock. The bow was held away from the dock by a heavy line from a mooring anchor on the seabed out toward the harbor entrance. Then a second row of yachts was placed in front of the first row. These had long stern lines to the same dock and their bows held toward the harbor entrance with mooring lines. Outboard of the second row was a *third* row of sailing yachts and power vessels with their bows held away from the dock with mooring lines and very long stern lines that went to the dock.

In order for someone in the second row to leave or enter, the third row had to be moved. For the first row, it meant both the second and thirds rows had to be moved. When someone in the third row went out for the day and returned, the long stern lines to the dock had to be hand-carried past the second and first rows. The confusion of mooring lines and stern lines was a nightmare.

I was about to leave the harbor and anchor off the beach outside when a man in a small launch appeared alongside and handed me a bow mooring line. Another fellow on the second row on our port side threw us a line, and as I looked, a man on the second row on our starboard side motioned for a stern line. Another member of the team was adjusting fenders on the intervening yachts. I had been introduced to *ormeggiatori* or the professional mooring managers of Italian yachting. Harbor too small? Too many boats?

Hire the ormeggiatori to sort things out and keep order. Ready to go sailing for a few hours? Alert the ormeggiatori. Worried about security? Slip one of the ormeggiatori 10,000 lira and emphasize one of your eyes by touching a cheek with a forefinger and the man would nod gravely. Need a letter sent or help with a grocery delivery? The ormeggiatori were always on hand.

We learned that the harbor had been built for 200 small yachts, but 400 small vessels had been shoehorned in. In spite of my reservations about the ormeggiatori and the tiered mooring system it all seemed to work. The men did a creditable job, and the patrons accepted them as part of the scene.

Occasionally the spectators on the dock got a little excited at all the line handling. Then the people in the dock chorus would shout and wave their arms and offer advice. Or cluck their tongues and shake their forefingers in disapproval. After all this was Italy and one had to expect a little *Il Trovatore* or *Il Barbiere di Siviglia* on a sunny Sunday morning.

We collapsed in our bunks and slept. Four hours later we went ashore to have a look at Circe's island. As I said earlier the so-called island is the south-facing elevated end (Cape Circeo) of a peninsula that juts into the sea from the mainland, which here is low and swampy. The highest point on Circe is 541 meters and roughly three miles in diameter with steep cliffs on the west and south.

These days Circeo is a pleasant resort area for people from Rome. Visitors whip down in flashy BMWs and pastel-colored Alfa-Romeos to spend a few days on their boats or in vacation homes.

The old part of San Felice village is up on a steep hill with winding streets and houses with balconies and terraces high above the sea.

The hill is cool and inviting with shady trees and carefully-clipped shrubs accented here and there by the shimmering reds of azaleas and bougainvillea. For an afternoon we sampled the edge of an upscale world, and watched a parade of pretty summer finery on the chic women of Italy. Circe's name was everywhere: on hotels, restaurants, bars, coffee shops, taxicabs. We saw it on business cards during the day and flashing at night in neon. Maybe something from the goddess of ancient times has filtered down to present-day Circeo.

Instead of the oaks that Odysseus saw, today the summit of Mt. Circeo is an antenna farm.

A road wound through a thick forest to the highest point of the island. From the top the open sea stretched away to the west; to the south we could see the tiny islands of Ponza, Palmarola, and Zannone seventeen miles in the distance. To the north of us lay the Pontine marshes, a maze of shimmering lagoons and small rivers. Once the marshes were wild and good for hunting; now they've been mostly drained and are intensively farmed. Yet in places there are forests of oaks, pines, oleasters, and arbutus.

But where was Circe? The temptress with the magic wand and suspicious goodies for passing warriors? Gods are supposed to be immortal and live for all time. Was she hiding around the next corner? Or was I once again chasing after a wraith in the sea, a fantasy, a paragraph in an ancient book? We tramped around this island of fantasy, but saw no real signs of Circe or over-friendly wolves or lions. We failed to find Circe's palace of dressed stone. We saw no gleaming doors or silver-studded chairs. We hefted no silver pitchers, no ewers of gold, or other Mycenaean treasures that Homer loved so much. We climbed through the pines to the top of the mountain and searched for a plume of smoke, but all we saw were television transmission towers, microwave relay stations, and the lighthouse far below. It was easy to imagine Circe, Eurylochus, and Odysseus acting out their noble tale on this pleasant peninsula. Maybe we were play-acting, but it somehow linked us to the world of long ago.

Looking northeast across the Galli Islands toward the Amalfi coast.

THE SIRENS, SCYLLA, & CHARYBDIS

F OLLOWING THE WRITINGS of the Greek geographer Strabo, the ancient Roman poets, and many classical scholars, we sailed southeast along the coast of Italy for 70 miles. This took us from Cape Circeo to Bocca Piccola, the strait between the island of Capri and the mainland. Then with the Gulf of Naples behind us we turned east-northeast and headed a few miles into the Gulf of Salerno. This brought us to the Galli islands, the home of the Sirens.

The weather had been rotten. Fickle winds blew from the north, and big seas thundered past us. Rain poured down. But the sky was clearing with patches of blue sky, and now and then we could see the sun. In the distance the houses of Positano and Amalfi stood out as tiny rectangles of white against the steep green hills of the mainland.

The Galli islands are three tiny islands plus a few above-water rocks about a mile from the mainland. The largest islet—Gallo Lungo—has a handful of deluxe summer houses. When we arrived, the leftover swell from the storm was breaking on the islets and ringing them with white water. As we circled the islets I was so busy tacking and gybing that I forgot all about the legend of the Sirens. Margaret stood in the main companionway inspecting the islands with the binoculars.

"Listen!" she said. "Do you hear those lovely voices enticing you closer to the rocks? Closer and still closer? Shall I bind you to the mast?"

I cocked my head and listened carefully for those spellbinding human voices—or any voices at all. (Would they be in Italian or Greek? Or was I being too literal again?) All I heard was the cry of seagulls and the crunch and slop of the waves on the rocks. The Sirens might have been there, but perhaps they were sleeping. I thought of the famous orange-on-black Greek vase in the British museum in London that shows Odysseus tied to the mast while his men—their ears plugged with beeswax—row onward. Above the Greek ship one of the Sirens—half-human, half-bird—floats in the air like a figure in a Chagall painting, singing sweetly as she tries to coax and bewitch Odysseus to her deadly lair where the bones of her victims lie heaped up. Two other bird-Sirens wait on nearby rocks.

What song did these sweet charmers sing? The heroic couplets of Alexander Pope's translation of 1725 roll the words off nicely:

> O Stay, oh pride of Greece! Odysseus stay!
> O cease thy course, and listen to our lay!
> Blest is the man ordain'd our voice to hear,
> The song instructs the soul, and charms the ear.
> Approach! Thy soul shall into rapture rise!
> Approach! And learn new wisdom from the wise.
> We know whate'er the kings of mighty name
> Achieved at Ilium in the field of fame;
> Whate'er beneath the sun's bright journey lies,
> O stay, and learn new wisdom from the wise . . .[33]

Could the sucking and gurgling sounds that waves make when they roll across shoreline rocks with holes and cracks in them have been confused with the sounds of human voices? Or were the islands of the Sirens simply the human junkyard for misbegotten wishes and foolish urges?

LIKE ODYSSEUS WE SQUARED OFF and headed for the Strait of Messina, 150 miles to the south-southeast, and sped along before a fair wind from the northwest. Little by little we pulled offshore. I was glad when the ironbound Italian coast dropped below the horizon because we were much safer at sea than heading along a lee shore with rocks and cliffs and marginal harbors. Also we were

Everyone has seen photographs of the British Museum's famous fifth-century Greek vase from Vulci. The artist shows Odysseus bound to the mast while his men—their ears plugged with beeswax—row doggedly onward. Two bird-sirens trill sweet words and promise paradise to the men while a third flies near and does maneuvers above the ship. Odysseus has been warned that the sweet words will lead him to his death, but once he hears them he begs to be set free. His men only bind him more tightly. Soon the ship is past the danger.

able to steer a straight course toward our target rather than to follow an irregular coastline.

While I was congratulating myself on my good judgment the wind changed abruptly to the east-southeast. An hour later I had two reefs in the mainsail, the 110 percent jib strapped in tightly,

Gallo Lungo, Galli islands.

and we were banging along at 5.3 knots under low clouds and light rain. (The apparent wind was 24 knots at 35°.) We were making reasonable time but getting blown off to leeward a bit which meant that we'd either have to tack or we'd wind up among the Eolie islands on the north side of Sicily. This didn't worry us because the easternmost island of the Eolie group was Stromboli, an active volcano that's visible for miles.

Both on an earlier trip and during the twenty-six months in the Mediterranean that we chased after Odysseus we noticed that the season of fine weather changed abruptly at the beginning of September. The winds became more capricious and stronger. Often they arrived unannounced in spite of lots of talk from weather forecasters who, notwithstanding their satellites and computer models, were no better than weather reporters. On one run westward from Crete we dutifully wrote down the daily forecasts for eighteen consecutive days. Fifteen of the eighteen forecasts were wrong, often dramatically so.

I believe the information is available, but the weather people fail to deliver it to vessels concerned with surface winds or to use the resource of raw data from the ships themselves.* The truth, I suppose, is that compared to the millions ashore, who cares about fishermen and a few nuts on sailing yachts? Additionally, the Mediterranean forecasts are difficult because local land winds and the seaside topography strongly influence what happens on the surface of this great inland sea. Where else in the world is there a body

---

*Herb Hilgenberg, a private weatherman in Canada, delivers first-class forecasts by integrating information from the target ship.

of water that's 2,400 statute miles long and in places only 90 miles wide with irregular mountains on the north and burning deserts on the south? No wonder the ancients always laid up their ships during the winter months and sacrificed animals to the weather gods.

In going south from Circeo, Odysseus would have stuck to the shore and hunted for places to beach his ship when the wind was against him or the men were tired. Because of the indented coastline, however, he would have sailed at least 225 miles and taken a lot of time at each stop. (Remember that he liked to explore and investigate strange places.)

In sailing or rowing, the Greeks would have logged about 30 miles a day—ten hours at three knots. The trip that needed 30 hours on *Whisper* would have taken the ancient vessel a week or more even if the men from Ithaca had sailed overnight a few times. In the 19-knot headwind that we encountered, Odysseus would have stayed ashore.

Odysseus must have been curious about the lands ahead. On *Whisper* we knew exactly where we were going and the distance to the next port. We had the help of our wonderful magnetic compass, a device that modern sailors take for granted, but really should worship like the Holy Grail.

The wind backed to the east, and we speeded up a little. Stromboli appeared right on schedule. It was an enormous black cone three miles in diameter and 3,000 feet high that smoked and fumed and puffed and sent a stream of cinders into the sodden morning sky. The mountain truly seemed alive and dangerous and out of a horror movie. Yet we could see a small village on the western shore. Certainly Stromboli was a strange place on which to live. Somehow after all the talk and hype about this so-called "beacon of the ancients" in the history books I was a little disappointed. As a navigator I would say that Stromboli is a useful checkpoint when going south, but not much more.

Some people believe that Stromboli and a tiny nearby volcano called Stromboliccio are the Wandering Rocks that Circe mentioned as an alternative route. Odysseus, however, elected to bypass the Wandering Rocks (sometimes called the Clashing Rocks) and continued toward Scylla and Charybdis.

In both ancient and modern times there's been plenty of con-

This handsome purse seiner is working off the waterfront of Scilla. Unfortunately the fish are small. The six men have to split the catch and give extra shares to the captain and make an allowance for the boat and her gear.

troversy about Homer and *The Odyssey* but not about the location of the female monster that devours sailors and the whirlpool that threatens ships. Even people who have never read a word of Homer know the meaning of "between Scylla and Charybdis." My American Heritage dictionary says: "Charybdis. *Greek Mythology.* A whirlpool off the Sicilian coast, personified as a ship-devouring sea monster and located opposite the cave of Scylla."

Aboard *Whisper* our favorable wind continued. The rain had increased and seemed to beat down the seas. We probably had some south-setting tidal stream with us because Stromboli soon disappeared astern. In the late afternoon high land appeared ahead: Sicily to the right, the Italian mainland to the left. As we approached the Strait of Messina, we began to see large and small ships, first one or two, then a dozen. Just before dusk we anchored

---

*For unknown reasons, the fishing village is spelled Scilla or in older times Sigla. Homer's sea monster in the cave is spelled Scylla.

off the fishing village of Scilla* on the east side of the strait near its northern entrance. We hung up a bright anchor light, had dinner, and turned in early. It had been a long day.

The next morning when I looked out at dawn, the fishermen, working in the dim shadows below a large cliff, were preparing their gear and helping one another slide their small boats into the water. We had breakfast, launched our dinghy, and rowed ashore.

Scilla (population 5,555) lies on the side of a steep, north-facing mountain that plunges into the sea. The dwellings cling to the rocky slope and seem ready to slide downhill and disappear into the water. But somehow they hang on. A few of the fishermen have homes that front directly on the sea, and they drag their boats up on skids between the houses. Silkworms and mulberry trees are raised in the district, and some of the people extract perfume oils from citrus fruits. Others cultivate grapes and make wines.

However Scilla's real claim to fame is a tall, cliff-like thumb of rock that extends seaward from the mountain at the west end of the harbor. According to Homer a cave partway up this rocky tower is the home of a horrible six-headed female monster (with twelve writhing legs and three rows of terrible teeth on each head) who

Fishermen preparing small boats, Scilla.

snatches passing sailors from their ships and gobbles them up after first terrifying them by her appearance.

Whether or not the monster exists, there are several caves, called *dragara*, at water level in the base of the thumb. As sea water is forced in and out of these openings it makes scary and unnerving sucking and moaning sounds. [34]

As we walked around Scilla, Margaret and I peered up at this smooth thumb of rock, which we estimated was 250 feet high, depending where you measured. We saw no caves. No lurking monsters. However the phantoms of the past may have been exorcised by the knights who constructed a castle on top of the thumb or by the priests who later built a church on top of the castle.

Scilla has a tiny harbor, but any wind or swell from the north or northeast rolls into it. The fishing is done from small open boats usually driven by one-cylinder inboard diesel engines; all have oars that the men use as well. The carvel-planked wooden boats are about twenty feet long and nicely maintained. Most are painted a light shade of blue with white, black, and yellow trim.

A majority of the fishermen—wise to the ways of the sea—pull their boats up on shore when they're not in use. When the men come in from fishing they row into the harbor, lift out the rudder, and ground their boats in shin-deep water at the edge of a concrete ramp. Then barefoot—everyone is barefoot—they step out and snap a hook to the bow from a six-part tackle that runs up on the ramp and haul their boats out of the water. The fish the men bring in are often pathetically small, but they persevere day after day and scratch out a living. Most of the fishermen we saw were middle-aged, which suggests—like elsewhere—that most of the young men head for the big cities.

As we watched old men sitting in the sun and children laughing and shouting as they raced up and down the narrow lanes, I had the feeling that the life style of this village had been unchanged for generations—for hundreds, perhaps thousands of years. The place had an air of ordered pace, a steadiness, perhaps a bit of resignation. The village might have been rough and poor, but it had dignity and permanence.

Homer tells us that Scylla not only gobbles up men but eats swordfish and dolphins as well. This gives us another clue that

The tower of Scilla, supposed home of the six-headed female monster with twelve grasping legs and multiple rows of sharp teeth on each head.

ties his work to the Strait of Messina. Large numbers of swordfish are found in only a few places in the Mediterranean. The swordfish business in the strait has been known from time immemorial, so long in fact that the Italian and Sicilian fishermen have evolved special boats and techniques. So-called "water rights" to certain fishing areas along the strait are handed down from father to son, and probably enforced in ways I don't want to think about.

When I first saw a swordfish boat I didn't know what it was. I thought it must have something to do with oil well drilling or pile driving. But none of these notions made the slightest sense.

I saw an open wooden boat about 35 feet long with a seventy-foot steel lattice mast and a bowsprit as long as the boat. A mass of wire stays and shrouds supported the mast and bowsprit. I eventually learned that these strange vessels are built solely for the taking of swordfish and generally go out from April to June, the best months.

The top of the mast is simply a platform for the captain who is also the lookout and who gives all the orders. The harpoonist operates at the end of the bowsprit. Two men deal with the harpoonist's line and another crewman handles the engine while the boat, guided by signals from the captain aloft, glides silently up to a swordfish basking on the surface. The man with the harpoon does his work and quickly belays the line from the harpoon to a strong point. The swordfish, sometimes 10-15 feet long and weighing up to 450 kilos (but taken commercially at half this size), either sounds or races off and tows the boat behind. But the effort is hopeless, and the fishermen soon bring the valuable fish alongside, haul it on board, kill it, and whack off the sharp, elongated upper jaw. This all sounds exciting and profitable, but the men work long hours and are soon burned black from the glare of the summer sun while they stalk their next victim.

ACCORDING TO HOMER, as Odysseus approached the Strait of Messina, Scylla—the female monster—lurked on one side. Charybdis hovered on the other. As soon as Scylla saw the ship she snatched six men from the crew—one man with each of her six heads. Meanwhile Odysseus and the thirty-eight men who were left—terrified that they'd be next—pulled like demons to get away from Scylla. They escaped, but the extra speed of the ship put them in the grasp of Charybdis. Now the ship had to run the gauntlet of the black swirling water. It was the old story of a person jumping sideways to avoid trouble and stepping into something worse.

The ancients dreaded the Strait of Messina. A particularly bad accident happened in the early fifth century B.C. A boat going from Messina to Rhegion with thirty-six choir boys, their teacher, and a flutist capsized. Everyone was drowned. The people on both sides of the strait were horrified. To mark their sorrow the elders of the two cities erected a splendid monument in Olympia.

The strait was the home of a thousand terrors—strange fish, terrifying squalls, waterspouts, vicious tidal bores, and worst of all—Charybdis. *The Odyssey* says that three times a day the whirling maelstrom sucked away the water until an observer could see the black sands on the floor of the strait. Three times a day Charybdis vomited upwards and flung out steam and boiling water in all directions, like a cauldron boiling over on a blazing fire. Charybdis meant disaster for any nearby ships.

So much for the ancient tale. In modern terms the story is this:

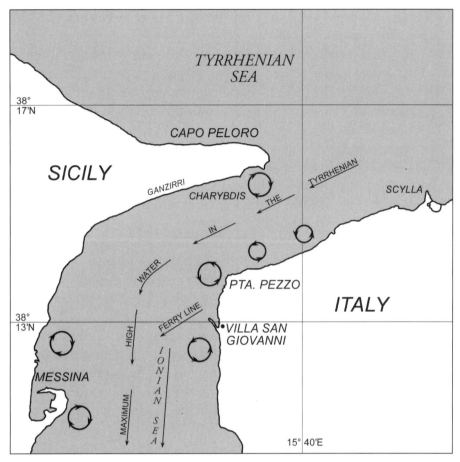

STRAIT OF MESSINA

The movements of the sun and moon in relation to the earth cause tidal flows. The Mediterranean, however, has little tidal action except in a few places. One of these is the Strait of Messina, which links the Tyrrhenian Sea to the north and the Ionian Sea to the south.

At Cape Peloro at the northern entrance to the strait on the Sicilian side, the tidal stream acts like the waters of the Tyrrhenian. A little over two miles south at Punta Pezzo on the Italian coast, the sea acts like the Ionian. However the times of high and low water of the Tyrrhenian and the Ionian are about six hours apart. This means that when it's low water at Punta

Pezzo, it's high water at Cape Peloro. Six hours later the highs and lows reverse.

So roughly four times each day the water slopes from the Tyrrhenian to the Ionian or from the Ionian to the Tyrrhenian. We're only talking about a one-foot maximum tidal difference, but because the water is forced into the 1.8 mile-wide channel between Punta Pezzo and a place called Ganzirri on the Sicilian shore, the water sweeps through the strait at up to 4¼ knots. North and south of this area the tidal streams quickly weaken. In addition, the Ionian Sea is colder and saltier than the Tyrrhenian. This sets up a south-flowing surface current of ¼ knot that can increase to one knot in brisk northerly winds.[35]

The bottom is extremely uneven in the narrow part of the strait and varies in depth from 200 to 1,200 feet. This contributes to tidal rips and eddies that flow contrary to the main stream. Ninety feet down, for example, the south-going current reverses itself and flows northward.

Each time the tide changes, there's a period of slack water for a few minutes. Then the water commences to flow, beginning with a tidal bore or "Taglio," which is a small wall of water followed by swirls and minor whirlpools. A second "Taglio" comes an hour later, with breakers that can be five feet high.

> "With the N-going stream the second 'Taglio' is often not very remarkable, but with the S-going stream it can be an imposing spectacle," states the tenth edition of the British Admiralty Pilot book, the authority on the area. " . . . If the wind is blowing against the advancing 'Taglio' the short high seas formed may become dangerous to small craft."[36]

All these movements of water overlap and are complicated by countercurrents and winds. Whirlpools, overfalls, and great ripplings are commonplace. Today some of these eddies even have special names, which date back hundreds of years. With the south-going stream from the Tyrrhenian the water is thermally stable. But with the north-going stream, the colder and denser water from the Ionian rises to the surface and brings up strange fish from great depths. (Ten miles south the soundings go to 3,282 feet.) The legend of the monster of Scylla may have some connection with a giant squid, a hammerhead shark, or other unusual sea creatures. No wonder the ancients were terrified by the Strait of Messina.

Today, of course, enormous ships with colossal diesel engines or turbines with thousands of horsepower serenely power through the strait and scarcely give the place a thought. The fishermen of Scilla, in their twenty-footers, are more respectful.

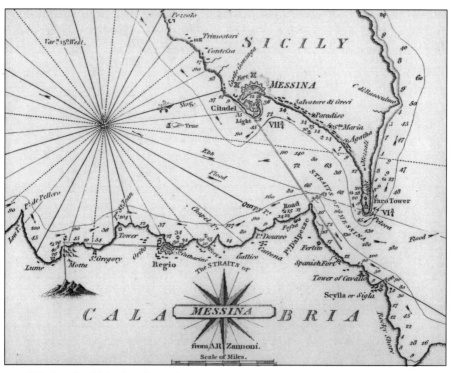

*The Strait of Messina from the 1821 British Pilot book. Note that this plan (by
A. R. Zannoni) is drawn with west toward the top (up) and north to the right.
A Spanish fort is shown on the east side of the narrow part of the strait; Messina
has both a fort and a citadel. The prominent point just south of the narrows
(on the east side) is called Punta Dalpesze; today it's known as Punta Pezzo
(photograph on page 150), perhaps a corruption of the earlier name.*

THE CATTLE
OF THE SUN GOD

O NCE PAST THE PROBLEMS in the northern part of the
Strait of Messina, Odysseus hurried southward.
The waterway widened out, and the current and
tidal stream fell away to nothing. The ship was finally in the
Ionian once more, the sea that led to Ithaca. Ah, wonderful
Ithaca. Would they ever see that fair land again?

The men still hadn't recovered from the ghastly experience with Scylla when the monster had come down from her
cave, seized six of their fellow oarsmen, and—while the men
screamed and writhed—ate them like so many sausages. The
ship then narrowly avoided catastrophe in the black pit of
whirling Charybdis. But now things were better, and the men
pulled at a steady stroke to get clear of the strait. Early on
they passed the great hook of land on the Sicilian shore that
forms the harbor of the modern city of Messina. They could
have stopped there, but it was early in the day and the place
was only five miles from the terrors behind them.

They pressed south-southwest along the northern part of
the eastern shore of Sicily for another twenty-five miles, and
after a long day and a little help from the wind finally reached
Taormina (whose name is based on the Greek word *tauros*
for bull). This place is really the first possible stop for a small
vessel because from Messina the coast of Sicily is high and
bound by cliffs.

Thrinacia, another of Homer's elusive destinations, lay west of the anchorage. Thrinacia was the place where seven flocks of sheep and seven herds of cattle (each with fifty animals) feasted on tall grasses and clear mountain water. The animals belonged to Helios, the sun god. His two daughters, the nymphs Lampetie and Phaëthusa, looked after the cattle and sheep.

Odysseus wanted to keep going and bypass Thrinacia and all its problems, but the men groaned with fatigue and hunger. Eurylochus, always a troublemaker, spoke up:

"Master, you're tougher than the rest of us. You never get tired. We're exhausted. We want to walk ashore and stretch our legs, have a hot meal, and sleep. Out here in the dark a high wind could capsize the ship. With respect, let's start out again in the morning when we can see what we're doing."

When the men heard this they applauded.

"Very well," said Odysseus. "We'll stop, but you all must promise not to kill any of the cattle or sheep in Thrinacia. You must be content with the food that Circe gave us for the journey."

Everyone agreed. The sailors then anchored the ship in the cove, went ashore, prepared supper, and slept. A little before dawn, however, a gale blew up from the south, so as soon as it was light, the party dragged the ship ashore to keep her from pounding and breaking up.

For the second time Odysseus warned his men not to touch the cattle or sheep. "Remember these are special animals that belong to Helios, the sun god. His daughters Lampetie and Phaëthusa keep a close watch over them."

Once again everyone promised not to touch the animals. The season of fair weather was over, and the cursed south wind continued to blow hard for an entire month. At first everyone was pleased to rest and eat the food and drink the wine from the ship. But as the weeks passed the provisions began to give out. The men were hungry and spent their time fishing or trying to snare birds or game. One day Odysseus walked off by himself to pray to the gods on Mt. Olympus for help. After his prayers, he fell asleep.

In the meantime Eurylochus stirred up the men.

"Starvation's a miserable end," he said. "Let's butcher some of the sun god's cattle and sheep. To make amends we'll build a special temple to the sun god and put in plenty of rich offerings when we get back to Ithaca. If the sun god doesn't like it and sinks our ship beforehand at least it will be a quick death. It's better than slow starvation here."

When Odysseus awoke and smelled the roasting meat he was horrified. But it was too late. The damage was irreversible. Helios, the sun god, flashing overhead, soon found out what had happened from his daughter Lampetie who had seen everything from close up. He was furious and ran to Zeus, crying for vengeance. The king of the gods was outraged. He sympathized with Helios and swiftly passed judgment.

"I'm going to destroy the ship of Odysseus with a fierce thunderbolt," he said.

The men from Ithaca feasted on the forbidden cattle for six more days. On the seventh the wind died down. The sailors quickly launched their vessel and set off again, but as soon as they were out of sight of land a hurricane-force wind from the west pounded into the ship. The mast toppled backwards and killed the helmsman. Then a great shaft of zigzag lightning split the sky; a huge wave capsized the ship and tore her to bits. The men were thrown into the sea and soon disappeared.

Odysseus managed to grab the leather backstay, which was fastened to the mast, and used it to tie the mast and wooden keel together. He crawled up on this crude raft and somehow hung on. Now the wind changed to the south and blew Odysseus, still clinging to the wreckage, all the way back to Charybdis. He was sucked into the great whirlpool and flung out again. The wind died, and he drifted south for nine days. Finally the raft washed up on the island of Ogygia where the goddess Calypso lived.

The ominous prophecies of Circe and Tiresias had come true. The men had eaten the sacred cattle and perished. The last of the twelve proud ships was gone. Odysseus, broken, wretched, and miserable, lay on the beach. He was closer to death than life.

• • •

WE SAILED FROM SCILLA on October 1st. The weather was suspiciously good, and as I hoisted *Whisper's* mainsail I looked up at the sky and wondered how long the fair wind would last. A few minutes later we glided past the steep face of Homer's ancient cliff, which glowed a tawny yellow in the soft light of morning. I looked up again. Was Scylla in her cave? Did I see some movement up there? Or was I in fantasyland and hallucinating again? Certainly the story was a way the ancients had of explaining things they didn't understand. Did the Greeks use the myth of Odysseus to forecast their dreams about a faraway world in the same way that Americans think of the legends of Paul Bunyan, Santa Claus, and cowboys of the Old West?

Long before, while preparing for the trip, I'd copied down an excerpt from an old (1854) British Admiralty Pilot book. The warning made me nervous:

> Outside the . . . harbour . . . we see the Galofaro, or celebrated vortex of Charybdis, which has, with more reason than Scylla, been clothed with terrors by the writers of antiquity. To the undecked boats of the . . . [ancients] it must have been formidable; for, even in the present day, small craft are sometimes endangered by it, and I have seen several men-of-war, and even a seventy-four-gun ship (the *Queen*, bearing the flag of Rear-Admiral Sir Charles Penrose), whirled round on its surface; but by using due caution, there is generally very little danger or inconvenience. . . . The Galofaro appears to be an agitated water, of from 70 to 90 fathoms in depth, circling in quick eddies; but rather an incessant undulation than a whirlpool. . . . This agrees in some measure with the relation of Thucydides, who calls it a violent reciprocation of the Tyrrhene and Sicilian seas; and he is the only writer of remote antiquity I remember to have read, who has assigned this danger its true situation, and not exaggerated its effects.[37]

In any case our business that day was whirlpools, so we set off to look at rough water in the Strait of Messina. Would we be thrown ashore? Would we be swirled around and around and driven from our course? Would we be overwhelmed and sunk? I had the feeling that the hands of antiquity were on my shoulders.

The tenth edition of the Admiralty Pilot book (1978) identi-

The whirlpool of Charybdis on the west side of the strait. Along the shore in the distance is the Sicilian village of Ganzirri.

fies three major whirlpools in the strait, no doubt caused by the extremely uneven bottom and the colossal quantities of water that pour through this bottleneck four times each day.

The first is the famous Charybdis, which is three miles west of Scilla and just inside the northwest entrance to the waterway. (See sketch map on page 141.) Since we were headed south toward Taormina we decided to arrive at Charybdis during daylight and one hour before the south-going tide was at its maximum. (We were about halfway between spring and neap tides, the twice-monthly maximum and minimum tidal flows.)

The wind was from the north at ten knots; it took us about an hour to sail the three miles from Scilla because we had to go behind several big container ships that were speeding northward.

Since the strait has great depths and no rocks we headed boldly toward the Sicilian shore. A little to the right we could see a lighthouse and a spidery metal pylon (764 feet high) that until recently anchored one end of electric power cables that spanned the strait. Ahead of us was a village called Torre Faro.

Whirlpool at Punta Pezzo on the Italian (east) side of the strait.

Margaret was steering west and began to sense the tidal stream. "I can feel it. I can feel the power," she shouted above the noise of the water. "We're getting set along the shore. To the south-west. Look at the buildings along the shore!"

All at once there were hundreds of tiny breaking foot-high wavelets around us. Just ahead was a circular patch of water 100 or 125 feet in diameter (say three boat lengths) that was slowly revolving. Presumably this circle of water was Charybdis. What I saw was not a swirling rotational velocity (like water in the kitchen sink) but a smooth upwelling of water from the depths. The chart said the bottom was 864 feet down. I had no idea if this rising water was coming from that depth, but clearly there were big water movements down there somewhere. The water in the whirlpool looked almost oily, a sort of river in the sea, something like the eddies in the Gulf Stream north of Bermuda.

The water movement and the splashing wavelets outside the whirlpool made a lot of noise, but as we looked, the whirlpool near us vanished. A few minutes later another appeared a little way off. Twenty minutes later it disappeared. Then another slick appeared behind us, and so on. Some whirlpools were small (75 feet in diameter). Some were large (say 150 feet). We sailed around for an hour or so and didn't seem to be in the slightest danger, although the spring tides weren't due for another week.

The second whirlpool mentioned in the Admiralty Pilot is 650 feet west of Punta Pezzo which was across the strait and two miles south on the Italian side. With a fair wind and the tidal stream with us we reached the area in less than half an hour. An 85-foot red and white lighthouse marks the place. Again we found small overfalls and upset water surrounding large circular patches of slowly revolving smooth water.

We took a few photographs and sailed to the third whirlpool: near the beach south of Punta San Raineri next to the big commercial port of Messina on the Sicilian side. Messina is the main ferry port for Sicily, and a bustling parade of passengers, automobiles, and railroad cars flows back and forth to Villa San Giovanni on the mainland side. Near Raineri we again found the oily patches of upwelling water surrounded by small breaking waves and swirling eddies. These whirlpools—on the order of 75 feet—were smaller than at Charybdis and Punta Pezzo.

We'd seen the three whirlpools and found them less daunting than their reputation, but they were at perhaps half strength when we sailed south. Apparently in former times there was a substantial whirlpool close to the village of Scilla as well. According to our reading, in 1783 a violent earthquake altered the sea floor. It may have toppled some of Scylla's tower and changed the water patterns in the strait. According to the Admiralty Pilot, the whirlpool of Charybdis was spectacular in the old days.

I know that much of the west coast of south Italy lies on a major fault line. Earthquakes are frequent, and we've all read about the eruptions of Etna, Stromboli, and Vesuvius. The Lipari islands north of Sicily also have a live volcano, and when we sailed there on a side trip while looking into Aeolus and the Clashing Rocks we hated the reek of sulphur that lay over the small islands.

AT LAST WE WERE PAST Scylla and Charybdis. I was tired of whirlpools and swirling water and hoped for some easy sailing for a change. The light northerly wind continued, so I eased the mainsail to port, and poled out a jib to starboard. Margaret and I took turns steering a course of 215° while we watched the yellow cliffs of Sicily slip by about a mile to our right.

Six hours later *Whisper* was abeam of Mazzaro bay at Taormina. Above us on the cliffs rose the glittering hotels and restaurants of a major tourist center. Tiny Mazzaro Bay (wide open to the east) was crowded with rocks and large yachts, so we pushed on another two miles south to the anchorage at Giardini. Just before dark we dropped a stern anchor and tied Whisper's bow to the inside of the short quay.

The next morning I slid back the hatch and looked out. Where was the island of Thrinacia? Where were the nymphs Lampetie and Phaëthusa? All I saw were hotels climbing the steep hills, beaches dotted with hundreds of umbrellas, naked bodies stretched out in the sun, and cars and enormous buses rushing along the coastal road. Where were the fine pastures? The tall green grasses? Where were the springs with the clear mountain water? I saw no fat sheep or wide-browed cattle. . . .

While I was thinking about events of 3,200 years ago, Margaret announced that the barometer was plunging.

"Yesterday afternoon it was 1014 millibars. Today it's down to 1008 and dropping."

Someone was pounding on *Whisper's* deck. It was the fisher-

The houses and hotels of Taormina from the anchorage near Mazzaro bay.

man whose boat lay next to us. He said that a southeast gale was imminent. He was worried about us bashing into his small boat. Would we please move?

I find it amazing how people who don't speak a common language manage to communicate when necessary. I thought the little harbor of Giardini was well protected from the south, but the locals would know. We moved out from the dock and anchored in the little bay behind the mole. During the night the front came through and a swell began to roll into the anchorage. We were reasonably situated, but another yacht that was farther out was pitching severely. Behind us on the beach the surf pounded into the shore. We knew that if the wind backed to the east we'd have to clear out. We put the dinghy on board and changed to a small jib. By daylight the barometer had dropped to 1004. Odysseus had the option of dragging his vessel ashore. Our draft was too deep, the hull shape too irregular, and the weight far too much for two people to deal with. Our options were to go out to sea or to a safe place, so we slipped out of Giardini and sailed seven miles south to Riposto, a large, well-protected harbor with substantial seawalls and a good-sized fishing fleet. Once inside we were safe. It was a working harbor; no tourists were in sight.

The next day the sky cleared, and we saw Mt. Etna for the first time. It lay ten miles inland, an enormous, bulky mountain with snow on its top and an ominous wisp of smoke streaming from the 10,663-foot summit.

The October weather had turned chilly. I pulled on a sweater and it felt good. A well-dressed retired fisherman named John Cammarata stopped to talk and came aboard for coffee. Later he drove us to a supermarket and his home where we met his wife. I asked about cattle and sheep. John immediately pointed toward the mountain. "A few kilometers up in the foothills," he said. "Some nice places. Lots of grass in the spring. Do you want to buy a side of beef? I can take you. Do you have a big freezer?"

"No, no," I said holding up my hand. "It's about something else."

Back at the yacht I rigged a hose from our water tanks to a spigot on the seawall. John shook his head and put a hand on his stomach. "No good," he said. "There's plenty of water from the mountain. But the old pipes are no good. You can't drink it."

Again and again in southern Italy, Margaret and I heard the same story. Plenty of water but for washing only. The national government in the north appropriates money for new water systems in the south, but the Mafia controls the construction companies. Result? Token work, little improvement, the money gone, and bad water. Everyone drinks expensive bottled water.

John took me up the mountain a few kilometers to a spring where I filled *Whisper's* jugs with excellent water from Mt. Etna. As soon as we drove a little west we left the cliffs and rocky shoreline behind and came to vineyards and grasslands with sheep and cattle. Here, perhaps, was the Thrinacia of the ancients. Homer described Thrinacia as an island, but I believe the place is fanciful because he never saw Sicily or Italy.

There's a curious parallel between two parts of *The Odyssey*. When Odysseus sailed from Troy to the land of the Cicones in

Thrace (see chapter 5) he must have gone right past Samothráki. Yet Homer never mentions this prominent island with its cone-shaped mountain. In this chapter his character Odysseus sails past mighty Etna and stays on nearby Thrinacia for a month. Yet Etna—big and looming to the west—doesn't get a word. Clouds may have covered the mountain part of the time, but certainly in a month there would have been some clear days. This suggests to me more than ever that Homer never visited southern Italy and Sicily, but—as I've said elsewhere—wrote his story from reports by travelers and sailors. Yet we believe that Homer lived in the eastern Aegean. How could he not have mentioned the mountain on Samothráki? It's another unanswered mystery.

Some people believe that Homer didn't describe the mountains because he was blind and couldn't see them. That he dictated an imaginary story to scribes. Yet writing was in its infancy, a new language—perhaps like computer languages are today. In 750 B.C. who could have been skilled enough to take dictation? What did a scribe write on? On parchment or paper that hadn't been invented? On Egyptian papyrus that might have circulated in the Aegean? On clay tablets? There are dozens of unanswered questions . . .

WE WERE BOUND FOR MALTA, 123 miles to the south, but the autumn gales had begun. Yet after a nasty storm there were usually a few days of good weather. We watched the barometer, listened to the Italian weather reports, and to our friend John Cammarata, who had spent thirty-five years fishing in these waters.

John scorned weather forecasters. He based his predictions on the clouds over Etna. "If they're low and moving quickly south, it means that northeast winds are coming. If you see white clouds rising behind Etna, get ready for northwest winds. When the summit is hidden in clouds you can be sure of southwest winds. Finally, if the water level in the harbor is high, there will be a gale from the south."

I was so impressed with John's confident predictions that I thought his words should be chiseled into stone.

On October 6th we saw low water in Riposto's harbor and white clouds behind Etna. We left in a hurry. We sailed south past smoky

Catania, oily Augusta, and crowded Siracusa. By noon the next day we arrived at Capo Passero, the southernmost tip of Sicily, near an enormous complex of tuna nets. We had a southeast wind of ten knots and were sailing nicely. We had 55 miles to go.

[FROM THE LOG] 7 October. 1433 hours. One reef in the mainsail. Lumpy seas. 1535. Wind ESE 17. Second reef and three rolls in the jib. A vile sea quite out of keeping with this wind. I've tied the furling drum in place. 1635. Third reef in main and going at 6½ knots. 1738. Wind 26 knots from ESE. An occasional sea slops on board. The portlights are very clean. Incredibly there's a lovely sky of perfectly-spaced puffs of alto-cumulus. Almost a trade wind sky. 2040. Seven fishing boats and one ship in sight. Lightning and rain all around. A foul night. 2319. Hooray. We're in Valletta harbor and on the way to clear customs.

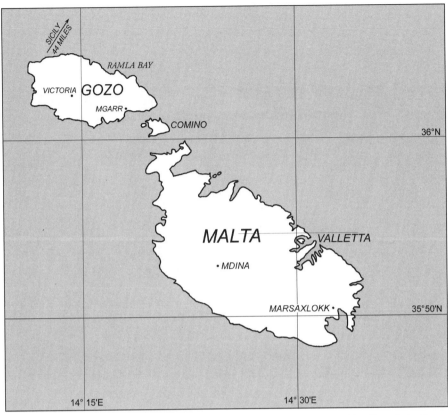

Malta is about 50 miles south of the southeast corner of Sicily and is directly in line with the east-west Mediterranean shipping lanes from which it derives some of its income. The capital is Valletta, one of the finest natural harbors in the world. The three islands total 122 sq. miles with a population of 370,000. Ruled by seven different countries in the past, Malta became independent in 1964. The people speak English and Maltese, a difficult form of Arabic. Our interest was Ramla bay on the north coast of Gozo.

Vase decoration, stag and billy goat. Caeretan hydria. Ionian workshop, c. 520–510 B.C.

THE CAVE
ON GOZO

ALYPSO DISCOVERED ODYSSEUS, unconscious and half-
dead, clinging to the wreckage of his ship as it washed
ashore on her island. Somehow she managed to drag
the battered sailor up the slope to her big cave where she and
her maids put him to bed. They washed him, fed him, covered him, and let him sleep. The next day he was a little better. Calypso fed him more thick soup and bits of beef. Soon
he was sitting up. Then he took a few steps. As the itinerant
mariner recovered, the nurse began to look at her patient more
and more. Somehow the immortal nymph Calypso, an elegant
and desirable goddess who was tied to no man, had met a
mortal named Odysseus and had fallen in love.

It was a poor match for Odysseus because he thought only
of Ithaca and his wife and son, but he was practical enough
to move in with Calypso and accept her hospitality and love.
Calypso believed she'd found a husband who would love
her and cherish her forever. She also knew that he'd stay
with her because he was stuck on the island and had no other
choice.

They lived together for seven years. But as time went on,
Odysseus grew increasingly melancholy and dejected. He
spent most of his afternoons sitting along the shore, quietly
sobbing and looking northeast toward Ithaca. He really
couldn't blame Calypso because who can complain when a

woman's only fault is to project her love and affection and to share her home and dinner table.

In any case there was no way Odysseus could leave Calypso's island of Ogygia because he had neither ship nor crew. He might have stolen a fisherman's boat, but Homer mentions no other people or ships on this will-o-the-wisp island.

At this moment the gods met in solemn session on Mt. Olympus. Everyone was there except Poseidon, who was away on business. The mighty Zeus, king of the gods, pre-sided. During the meeting Athena spoke of poor Odysseus who still hadn't returned to his loved ones after ten years of trials and wandering. Athena told how young Telemachus, his son, was threatened with death by Penelope's suitors when he returned from Pylos and Sparta where he had gone seeking news of his father.

Athena accused Zeus of indifference.

"Don't get excited, my child," replied the king of the gods. "It's Poseidon who's the problem. However I think we can work around him. In any case, it was your plan for Odysseus to return to his home and punish the suitors. With regard to young Telemachus, go ahead and use your ingenuity to pro-tect him."

Zeus then turned to Hermes and instructed him to go to Calypso and tell her that Odysseus was to go home forth-with. He was to travel by himself on a raft of his own mak-ing. His voyage would be arduous and full of trials, last twenty days, and end at the rich country of the Phaeacians. The rulers there would welcome him, present him with splendid gifts, and take him to Ithaca by ship.

The god Hermes laced on his magic sandals, picked up the wand of enchantment, and raced across the sea to far-off Ogygia. He found Odysseus down on the shore. Above the beach a grove of lovely shrubs and trees and vines framed the mouth of the cave. Birds flew all around, and flowers and herbs grew in thick clumps. As Hermes entered the cave he could hear Calypso singing in a heavenly voice while she worked at her loom. When she looked up and saw him she recognized him at once because all the immortals know one another.

After ambrosia and nectar, Hermes told Calypso what Zeus had decreed: Odysseus was to leave at once and journey to the land of the Phaeacians. He was to sail on a crude raft and make a twenty-day journey that would be marked with strife and pain. The people on the distant island would accept him on a high level and send him to Ithaca with bronze and gold and many gifts. Finally he would meet his loved ones.

When Calypso heard these cruel words she was devastated and complained bitterly. She had wanted to make Odysseus her lawful husband, but the jealous gods would not allow it.

"Now I must push the man I love out of my life because no goddess, no immortal can evade the will of Zeus even if I tried to do what was right."

After Hermes left, Calypso hurried out to Odysseus who was sitting near the shore. His eyes were rimmed with tears, for he felt that his life was ebbing away.

"Your grieving is over, my love," Calypso said, passing her gentle hand across his brow. "No longer do you have to sit here pining for your faraway land and family. I'm going to send you back. I want you to take this bronze axe and the shipbuilding tools and get ready to make a stout raft that will speed you across the flowing seas. I'll stock the raft with victuals and drink, and give you clothing and a fair wind."

Odysseus, tired of promises and wary of tricks, suspected foul play. He demanded a solemn oath that Calypso wasn't scheming some new bag of tricks.

The alluring goddess smiled at him and stroked his face. "Relax, dear Odysseus," she said. "I swear an oath to plot no tricks or intrigue. My heart is not made of iron. I will do for you what I'd do myself if I were in your shoes. Trust me."

Calypso led the way to her cave where she and Odysseus ate their last supper together.

"If you're still going to your beloved Ithaca, I wish you happiness," she said. "But I must warn you that you have terrible trials ahead. You'd be better off to stay with me. After all, aren't my face and figure better than those of a mere mortal?"

"Dearest Calypso," Odysseus replied. "Don't you think I know all this? You're tall and shapely. You have a lovely face and eternal youth. My problem is that I'm desperately home-sick. I must make another attempt to reach my home. If the sea swallows me I'll have to bear it somehow and try to go on."

The two then spent their last night together.

> When young Dawn with her rose-red fingers shone once more Odysseus quickly dressed himself in cloak and shirtwhile the nymph slipped on a loose, glistening robe, filmy, a joy to the eye, and round her waist she ran a brocaded golden belt and over her head a scarf to shield her brow then turned to plan the great man's voyage home.[38]

It was time to work. Odysseus took a great bronze axe, a fine adze, and all the other tools to the forest. He felled twenty trees and in a few days pinned them together into a first-class raft with a raised deck and bulwarks. While he stepped the mast and hoisted the yard, Calypso made a sturdy sail. She put aboard a sack of corn and fine meats along with skins of water and wine. Then she commanded a fair wind. Odysseus hoisted the sail and hurried back to the steering oar. The first singlehanded mariner sailed away. Homer doesn't say whether Calypso and Odysseus waved goodbye to each other, but let's hope they did.

CALYPSO HAD INSTRUCTED ODYSSEUS to keep the Pleiades, Arc-turus, and the constellation of Ursa Major (also called the Big Dipper, the Great Bear, or the Plow) close to port, that is 30°–40° to the left of his heading. This meant that Odysseus sailed northeast.

Unlike his swift, sleek warships the raft was squarish and slow, but the captain persevered. On his eighteenth day at sea he saw the mountains of Phaeacia (fee-AY-sha) ahead. The distance from Malta to Palaiokastritsa on the northwest coast of Corfu or ancient Phaeacia is about 335 miles. This translates to an average move of eighteen miles a day or three-quarters of a knot which is about right for a crude raft which would have encountered calms, cross-seas, rogue currents, and mostly very light west and southwesterly winds.

Now however, Poseidon, the god of the sea, back from his

foreign trip, looked down from the heavens and spotted Odysseus sailing northward.

"Look at Odysseus," grumbled Poseidon. "What did the other gods do while I was away? I'll fix that foxy sailor!"

Poseidon clapped the clouds together and hurled down a terrible blast of wind that whipped up the waves from every direction. Odysseus, in the eye of the tempest, knew that the warning of Calypso had come true. From every direction great waves hurled themselves at the tiny twenty-log raft. The king of Ithaca began to wish that he had perished at Troy where at least he would have received a hero's funeral. Out here in the screaming tempest there'd be no trace of him ever, only anguish.

A rogue wave capsized the raft, tore the weakened captain from the steering oar, and pummeled him and the raft from first one direction, then another. Odysseus thought it was all over, but help came in the form of Leucotha, the goddess of the sea's salty depths. She took pity on Odysseus and hurried to his side.

"Poor man," she said. "Why does Poseidon treat you so badly?"

She told Odysseus to take off all his clothes, leave the raft, and swim for the shore. Leucotha gave him a special divine veil to wrap around his waist that would protect him.

Poseidon's last move was to hurl down a final tempest that broke up the raft. In desperation Odysseus wound the veil around his middle and jumped into the roaring ocean. Athena now took a hand. She calmed all the winds except from the north. Odysseus fought the stormy waters for two more days and nights and thought he would surely drown. He was near land (to the east?), but the booming waves thundered on jagged rocks along the shore, and he feared that he'd be dashed to pieces if he went too close. Athena finally helped him find a beach clear of rocks where a river ran into the sea. In desperation he prayed to the god of the stream for help. The current in the river eased, and Odysseus, exhausted and half-dead, felt the bottom and staggered ashore. He crawled under some low trees, scraped a thick coat of leaves over his bleeding body, and slept.

The town and ferry port of Mgarr, Gozo. In the distance to the southeast lie Comino and Malta.

NORTH IN THE
IONIAN SEA

L IKE ODYSSEUS, Margaret and I left Malta and sailed for Corfu, far to the northeast. The date was June 9, 1997. We'd spent the winter in Malta and were ready to continue our search for the ancient Greek warrior. We'd painted and varnished and made various small repairs to *Whisper.* Now we loaded box after box of food aboard. Before heading into the Ionian Sea, however, we stopped at the nearby Maltese island of Gozo to see Calypso's cave.

We sailed to Ramla bay on Gozo's north coast, a quiet, isolated part of the eight-mile-long rocky island. In front of us lay a reddish beach called *Ir-Ramla I-Hamra*, backed by hills with a few deluxe summer houses and a series of low cliffs. The cave was somewhere near the top of the cliffs. We anchored, launched the dinghy, and Margaret rowed me ashore. The bay is open to the north, and though the winter storms were over, there were a few evil-looking clouds nearby. Margaret stayed on board to look after *Whisper.*

It was late morning and a dozen local families were on the beach. The children played in the sand while the men and women chatted in separate groups. The Maltese people are small in stature, slightly dark, speak Arabic, and in a pleasant way remind me of Spanish Gypsies. Since my Maltese consists of about five words I gambled everything on my first serve and walked up to three men.

"Bon-zhu. [good morning] Fayn oo [where is] Calypso?" This brought a few smiles, but also some arm-waving in the direction of the valley to the south and then to the ridge to the northwest.

I thanked the men who were farmers and whose small trucks were parked behind the beach. I set off up the valley, through fields of potatoes and tomatoes, and walked inland for a mile or so and then doubled back via a road that ran along the top of the cliff.

Meanwhile I thought about the reputed cave on which Homer based his story of Calypso—the tale of a woman who loved a man who loved someone else. It was the story of a goddess who offered to make the man she loved immortal, but who was overruled by Zeus, king of all the gods.

Homer spoke of a sweet-smelling fire of juniper and cedar in the cave, and Calypso singing while she worked at her loom. Grapevines grew at the entrance; nearby was a thick growth of alders, aspens, and cypresses—the home of owls, falcons, and crows. A series of springs bubbled a little distance away, and the water ran across meadows that were lush with flowers. According to the story, it was a wonderful place.

I soon arrived at the Ramla bay cave whose entrance is down a series of steps via a stone chute in the cliff. The cave itself faces the sea but is hard to see from a distance. The local story is that the cave was formerly much larger, but a substantial section of the front collapsed during an earthquake. The place is well-known and has been on tourist maps for a long time.

The caretaker was a local farmer who spoke a little English and German and who moonlighted for tourist tips. He lighted the cave with a dozen small white candles that he dotted around the walls. The yellowish flickering light suited the cave perfectly, gave an aura of ancient mystery, and made the cave surprisingly pleasant. Even the slight smoky smell of the candles seemed to fit the mood.

I saw the cave on a warm and sunny day. I was hot from walking, and it was peaceful inside. With the candles and the cool temperature the place seemed doubly inviting. I'd never thought about living in a cave, but why not? It doesn't take much imagination to put in a couple of rugs, a fireplace, a bed, and a little

The entrance to Calypso's cave and Ramla bay, Gozo.

furniture. You're protected from rain and wind and there's practically no upkeep. No painting. No taxes. No lawn care.

If this were the cave on which Homer based his story of Calypso, what was it like in ancient times? At that time Malta was probably heavily wooded and wetter. Today most of the trees have been cut down, much of the land converted to farming, and the general climate has become warmer.

ALTHOUGH I WAS INTRIGUED by the cave and it gave me a feel for the story, I was glad to signal to Margaret to pick me up in the dinghy. We were primed for the Ionian and anxious to visit Corfu and Ithaca. Once on board we hoisted the dinghy on deck, turned it over, and lashed it down over the coachroof. Then I cranked up the mainsail and the anchor. A minute later we set the jib and began to pull away from the land. The time was 1330 and our course was 050°. The distance to Corfu was 336 miles.

A weak breeze from the north barely ruffled the water. Could we sail so far in such light winds? A day earlier we'd left the Malta boatyard where we had carefully sanded and painted the bottom and installed a new Martec folding propeller. Close-hauled on the port tack, it didn't take much to move the yacht with her sleek bottom. We crept along at three knots or a little more like a smooth-swimming fish.

Since we were about to cross two major shipping lanes we kept careful watch for large vessels. It was rare that we had to take evasive action to avoid a ship, but someone had to be ready to change course. One of us was always in the cockpit trimming sails, adjusting the steering vane, and looking out for ships. We didn't have to do it every second, but the person on watch had to be on top of things. The other person was below and asleep, rattling around in the galley, or working at the navigation table.

Because of our self-steering gear we seldom had to steer manually, so a three- or four-hour watch meant mostly sitting in the cockpit and looking around. When we saw a ship we used a small hand-held compass to find out whether the ship's bearing stayed the same over a period of minutes. If that happened we changed course to avoid the other vessel, preferably going behind her. If we had a real problem we carried white phosphorus collision

Rowing ashore, Ramla bay.

flares which we could ignite in a second, but we have never used them.

We generally managed seven or eight hours of sleep in twenty-four although it was broken up. During the hours of darkness we stood three-hour watches, so in twelve hours a person would get six hours of sleep. In addition we generally took an afternoon nap. None of this was cast into stone, and often we called the other person if there was a problem (or crisis). I've found that if I sleep this way I need an extra hour or two because three two-hour naps aren't the same as six hours of uninterrupted sleep. In addition to sleeping we often relaxed in a berth with a book.

When we left Malta we had two or three large ships—container vessels, oil tankers, or bulk carriers—in sight at all times. The east-going were headed toward Suez; the west-bound for Gibraltar. That night a big sea-going tug passed us towing an enormous gray naval vessel (#108) that was blacked-out and ghostlike. The tug carried a rack of red and white lights that were bright enough so that I could see her stacks belching blue diesel fumes into the night.

> [FROM THE LOG] 10 June. 0932 hours. *Nora* of Constanta crossed close ahead. Another ship astern off Cape Passero at the SE extremity of Sicily. Light blue water. Depth 52 meters. Shore in plain sight. 1015. Tacked offshore. Wind ENE 7–8 knots. Speed 4.3. Our course is about 120°, not too good, but the wind will probably change as we work offshore to the east. 1040. A beautiful morning. A dozen Sicilian draggers working on the Malta bank. No big ships for the moment. Margaret is asleep. She's been looking better since we left Malta. Maybe the boatyard was getting her down.

During the day we sailed to the east and crossed the north-south shipping lane coming south from the Strait of Messina. Sicily disappeared behind us. Five smartly-painted Italian fishing boats passed us heading north, probably for Cape Spartivento. The wind gradually clocked around to the west and by evening we had a spinnaker up and were headed directly for Corfu. Now we were away from the major shipping lanes and able to relax a little. The toe of the Italian mainland was forty miles north. We knew the local shipping would stay within five or ten miles of the coast; nevertheless we kept a wary eye out for ships.

For dinner Margaret cooked a delicious meal of butterfly noodles and ham with cloves and nutmeg. We opened a bottle of red wine from Malta. Unfortunately it was poor, tasteless, vile stuff, most of which we poured over the side to appease the gods, although this wine might have angered them.

That night the sky was clear and the sea smooth; above me I could see hundreds of stars. Ursa Major (the Big Dipper) was overhead and a little to the north. Mighty Scorpio lay in the southern sky with yellowish Antares twinkling in the middle and Shaula, less bright and more bluish, toward the bottom of the long, skinny constellation.

Again and again I thought of Odysseus sailing northeast to the western Greek islands. I thought how he stayed on course by keeping Ursa Major (the Big Dipper) and Boötes (Arcturus) on his port bow as these great constellations wheeled round and round in the northern night sky.

Our light west wind continued all through the night, often falling away to a trace and then coming back. When the wind died, the spinnaker collapsed and made alarming swishing sounds. At first I rushed up to the foredeck ready to take down the sail, but a few puffs of wind came back, ballooned it out, and we carried on, rolling a little. In such light running winds the steering vane was useless because the apparent wind was close to zero, so we used a small electric autopilot that steered a straight, unwavering course. We paid back the batteries with the output from a solar panel during the day. What, I wondered, would the ancient Greeks have thought of these high-tech devices? Would they have considered them the earthly manifestations of the gods on Mt. Olympus?

We went on like this for three days while the mainsail slatted and the spinnaker struggled to keep full of wind. The noise from the sails was more disturbing than damaging because the fabric and stitching appeared quite unhurt. Our progress was hardly world-class racing, but in 72 hours we logged 195 miles and were only 90 miles from Corfu. It was amazing how we glided along on our magic boat with the red, yellow, and black spinnaker pulling us on and on across the quiet water. The spinnaker was our largest sail (930 sq. ft.) by far. Without it we wouldn't have gone anywhere in the light winds.

Occasionally a few shearwaters, dark-brown and slim, circled around us. Once we had a nervous, black-eyed pigeon on board. He (she?) was slim and pretty, but destined for the deep I feared. How did the bird ever get so far from land?

As we moved northeast in the Ionian Sea the weather grew hot and hazy. The visibility was poor, and when the sun was low in the sky it turned into a fiery orange ball. At night the air was damp. Moisture condensed on the sails and ran along the decks.

Light-weather sailing toward Corfu in the Ionian Sea.

The wind finally went around to the east. We took down the spinnaker and changed from the jib to the larger genoa. While we were kneeling on deck folding up the jib *Whisper* glided along at a couple of knots under the mainsail. The sea was quite smooth.

> [FROM THE LOG] 14 June. 1430 hours. While we were changing sails, I glanced over the side. We had come up on a swordfish sleeping (?) on the surface. About four feet long and so shiny that the fish seemed covered in silver tinfoil. He made a few movements and then shot away as the yacht neared him. It was my first swordfish. I was thrilled.

Now with an easterly wind and still on a course of 050°, we were on the starboard tack and hard on the wind. Fortunately the seas were easy, and we were headed for a weather shore. By noon the next day we thought we should be seeing land, but thick atmospheric haze veiled everything toward the east. Not until we were eight or ten miles offshore did we begin to see shadowy lumps, part of the big island of Corfu—ancient Scheria (SKEE-ree-a)—whose northwest-southeast dimension measured thirty-two miles. In two more hours the jigsaw puzzle ahead grew into a high, green island. Only fifteen years ago when we used sextants and mostly timed sun sights, it was sometimes tricky to make a landfall. We knew it was land but which land? From a distance most mountains and cliffs and hills tend to look the same. Is that Ace mountain or is that *not* Ace mountain? Experienced mariners know how easy it is to be wrong, and in the old days it was worth a bag of gold to have your exact position. Now it's all changed. Now with our magical GPS satellite navigation device, we read off our precise coordinates, and the headlands and bays showed up right on schedule. It was all too easy. Pity the ancient mariners and all those unnecessary wrecks.

By mid-afternoon we had slipped into the Paleokastritsa complex, a group of small bays, steep green cliffs, and distant hills on Corfu's northwest coast. We headed into the westernmost arm, which was a small bay named Limín Alípa. I dropped a stern anchor, and we tied *Whisper's* bow to a sturdy protecting mole. A Greek fishing boat lay to starboard. A yacht from England touched our port side. We had arrived at Homer's island of Scheria.

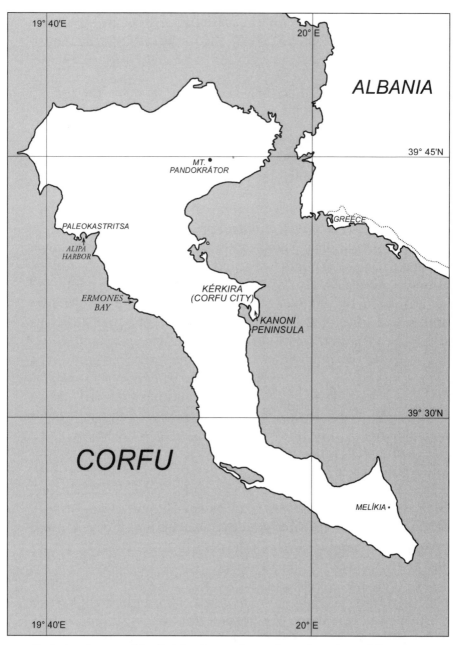

Corfu is a large and fertile island near the northwest boundary of Greece. Albania is only a few miles east of the northern part of the island. Note the narrow strip of Greek land along the southern border of Albania.

CORFU

T HE EXHAUSTED ODYSSEUS slept under a blanket of leaves beneath two olive trees on the shore of Phaeacia. Meanwhile the gray-eyed goddess Athena magically swept into the palace bedroom of Nausicaa, the lovely daughter of King Alcinous who was the local ruler. Athena had changed herself into a pretty sixteen-year-old friend of Nausicaa and while she slept, Athena spoke to her as in a dream.

Athena urged the young princess to wash all the fine clothes that lay neglected and dirty in her room. "Marriage season is at hand and you must dress in fresh things," said Athena. "I will help you. Ask your father for a cart and mules. Take your maids and all your family's soiled clothing to the river."

When Nausicaa (naw-SIH-kay-ah) awoke in the morning, she wondered about her dream, but straightaway went to her father and asked him for the high cart and two mules to take the laundry to the washing pools on the river. The king agreed, and her mother, Arete the queen, had a nice lunch prepared for her daughter and the maids. As the young women climbed into the cart, Arete gave Nausicaa a flask of olive oil so the girls could anoint themselves after bathing.

Off they went and after a time arrived at the river. They unhitched the mules so they could graze. Then the young women carried armloads of linens to the clear water pools where they soaked the clothing and jumped up and down on the fabrics to work out the dirt. When all the clothes were clean, Nausicaa and her maids spread them out on a shingle beach at the edge of the sea. Then they washed themselves, rubbed their skin with olive oil, and ate lunch. While they were waiting for the clothes to dry they began to frolic and play with a ball. When it fell into the water they shrieked and shouted as young women do.

The laughter woke up Odysseus, and he went to see who was there. Since he was naked he covered himself with a leafy branch he plucked from a tree. As soon as the maids saw a naked, wild-haired sailor streaked with salt and bits of seaweed they ran away. Only Nausicaa—to whom Athena had given an extra measure of courage—stood fast.

Odysseus began to talk to the young lady. "I've been ship-wrecked and need some clothing to cover myself," he said. "And directions to the city."

Nausicaa nodded. "We'll help you," she said, and introduced herself as the king's daughter. She called her maids and told them to wash and clothe the stranger. They took him to a sheltered place on the river and laid out a fresh cloak and tunic. In order not to embarrass the young women, Odysseus scrubbed himself and got rid of all the salt and scum. Next he anointed himself with oil and put on the fine clothing. Athena now stepped in and made Odysseus taller and more handsome.

When Nausicaa saw Odysseus she whispered to her maids that the man must be a god. "Oh that I should have such a person for my husband! But quick now, girls, give our guest food and drink."

Afterwards Nausicaa told Odysseus how to find her father's palace. To avoid the scandal of a princess being seen with a stranger, Odysseus traveled separately through the city, a busy place of ships and seamen.

The palace of King Alcinous (al-SEE-no-us) was a wonderful building of gold and silver and shiny bronze accented with glazings of blue. Marvelous sculptures of dogs guarded the entrance. In front lay magnificent orchards and vineyards and gardens watered by sparkling springs. Inside the palace fifty serving women hurried about grinding grain, spinning and weaving, and cleaning and keeping order.

Since the local people did not like strangers, Athena hid Odysseus in a magic fog so he could go through town unnoticed. Inside the palace the elders and ministers and guards didn't see him until he suddenly appeared in front of the astonished King Alcinous and Queen Arete. Odysseus told of the destruction of his last ship and how he had stayed with Calypso on Ogygia island for seven years before coming to Phaeacia and being rescued by Nausicaa. He begged for a ship to take him to Ithaca and home. The king agreed and promised a ship and gifts.

The next day there were sporting games, and Odysseus won the discus throw. Then came a grand feast. In the evening a bard sang about Troy. During the storytelling, King Alcinous spotted Odysseus weeping.

"Who are you, my friend?" asked the king. "Tell us about yourself. You seem no ordinary person."

"Who am I? Who am I? I am Odysseus, the king of Ithaca. The world talks of my schemes, and my fame has reached the heavens," he boasted.

Odysseus began to recount his adventures to the assembled group. He told about the Cicones, the Lotus-eaters, the Cyclops, Aeolus, and the Laestrygonians. Then his storytelling went on to Circe, the Land of the Dead, the Sirens, the Wandering Rocks, Scylla and Charybdis, and the Sun Cattle.

Since he had already spoken about Calypso, his twelve tales were at an end. Odysseus's sea chest had been filled with gifts from the Phaeacians, but King Alcinous was so impressed by his guest that he asked his people for valuable tripods—a special kind of trophy—as additional presents. His leaders agreed and a few hours later everything was loaded on the ship bound for Ithaca. Odysseus thanked his hosts and boarded the vessel, which made a quick trip to Ithaca. Odysseus, who was asleep, was gently laid ashore along with his gifts. Then the ship headed back. It seemed a miracle, but Odysseus had reached Ithaca.

• • •

MARGARET AND I SAILED to a lovely area on the northwest coast of Corfu. It was early summer, and Paleokastritsa was gorgeous, an interlocking series of coves, small bays, and offshore islets set amidst hills and high ridges that plunged into an ocean of shimmering blue.

Corfu is at the north end of the Ionian Sea next to the mountains of Albania and northern Greece. As a result the island receives more rain and is wooded, which means that you see the greens of pines and oaks and the silver-gray of olives everywhere. The trees were like old friends after the dry, barren islands and the heat of the southern parts of Italy and Greece.

In addition, the water was the clearest I've ever seen. I remember kneeling down and peering into the sea on the outer side of the mole in little Alípa harbor where we tied up *Whisper*. I couldn't believe the clarity of the water. In a depth of six meters I was able to see the bottom perfectly. As I looked, the water seemed to disappear, and I thought of words like pellucid, crystal, and limpid.

Because of beaches and the natural beauty, Paleokastritsa is popular with tourists. This means large hotels, crowds of people, and automobiles and buses. During our visit, however, nearby Albania had severe political problems and civil unrest because of a financial pyramiding scheme that had collapsed. Albanian refugees tried to flee to Italy and Corfu in a ragtag armada of falling-apart ships and decrepit fishing boats, which resulted in a hurry-up call for the Greek navy. All this trouble scared away half of the tourists.

This part of Corfu takes its name from Paleokastritsa monastery ("old castle"), which is located on top of a splendid isthmus site between two of the coves. The monastery was founded in 1225 A.D. and rebuilt at the end of the 18th century. The place is nicely painted in white, cream, and tan and has a fine bell tower and a splendid promenade beneath arches that alternate with trellises overlaid with vines. When I walked around the grounds, however, all I could think of was one question: Could the present monastery be on the site of the ancient Phaeacian city and palace of King Alcinous? Could the monastery be covering a Mycenaean ruin?

The clue in *The Odyssey* says that the city is ringed with walls with a fine harbor on each side. The wall—if there was one—is

The lovely area of Paleokastritsa on northwest Corfu.

long gone and might have been used for building materials for the monastery or for an earlier castle or fortification. Again and again I've seen places where medieval builders have constructed churches on what were considered pagan sites. In any case there's a reasonable harbor for small boats on each side of the present monastery.

It's hard to walk around Paleokastritsa and not think of ancient towns and villages in this easy-to-settle, pleasant area that has all of man's requirements. In addition to the monastery site there are half a dozen other nearby places where a Mycenaean settlement could have thrived. Unfortunately for the study of ancient cultures, enormous concrete-and-steel hotels have recently been built on top of all the likely sites—places no archeologist will be able to excavate. Tourist dollars, foreign exchange, and local employment rank infinitely higher than scientific inquiry. Perhaps in the future, archeologists will be able to investigate promising sites with x-rays or schemes yet to be invented.

Although there's little hard evidence, a number of investigators including the author Lawrence Durrell, who lived on Corfu for a time, and Victor Bérard, the eminent French scholar, have argued that the ancient Phaeacian city is somewhere in Paleokastritsa. The region seems ideally suited to a small, seafaring society, and if you tramp around the hills and bays you feel that Homer's lines describe this place perfectly. [39]

In truth, however, the ruins of the ancient Phaeacian settlement of King Alcinous are more likely to be on the *east* side of the island at modern Corfu's main city of Kérkira. To have a look at this place we sailed around the south end of Corfu and halfway up the east coast, a distance of fifty-two miles from Alípa harbor. When we arrived, the weather was settled so we anchored on the south side of the enormous medieval fort that juts into the sea from the center of the town. Behind us across Corfu channel lay the brown hills and mountains of Albania. There were six other yachts in the anchorage.

Ashore we found Kérkira, a town of 36,000, a charming place with elegant buildings, grassy esplanades, and intriguing small shops on horsecart-wide streets. Although the island has belonged to Greece since 1864, the town has many architectural gems that date back to the days of the Venetians, the French, and the British. Of the three foreign powers it was the Venetians who were in charge for more than four centuries and gave the place the gentle, relaxed flavor of Italy that exists today.

Immediately south of the present-day city of Kérkira is the Kanoni peninsula, which many think was the site of Homer's Phaeacians, but whose origins have been lost in the distant mists of time. The ancient city of Kérkira was supposedly founded in the eighth century B.C. However nobody is certain. Somehow Homer knew about the Phaeacians, their peninsula city that lay between two harbors, and their skill at seafaring. Later during the Peloponnesian War, Thucydides told about their seagoing exploits.

In modern times a few ancient ruins have been uncovered on the peninsula, which is mostly heavily wooded. However archeologists have never systematically explored the area. Part of the peninsula is a section called *Mon Repos* which has the old summer palace of the Greek Royal family. Prince Philip of England was born there in 1921. [40]

[FROM MY NOTEBOOK] 26 June. Yesterday we took a city bus around Kérkira and ended up at the south end of the Kanoni peninsula. We walked to a café high above the water and looked down at a wonderful view of a tiny church on a nearby islet with blue mountains in the distance. Were we at the home of old King Alcinous? Was this the same view that he enjoyed? As we sat quietly thinking about ancient times, the silence was shattered by the huge noise of a jet aircraft and a silver wing that slipped by us about fifty meters away. Ye Gods! The Greeks have built an international airport immediately behind the peninsula. The noise of the jets was horrendous. We gulped down our coffee and fled.

Margaret and I hiked all over the peninsula and Mon Repos which has been opened to the Greek people. The summer palace had been closed for years, and no one had touched the ornamental shrubs and trees for a long time. When we were there the palace was being totally rebuilt and squads of gardeners and tree experts were attacking the overgrown gardens and drives. We walked to the ruins of a large Greek temple, but it had tumbled down centuries ago, and the columns and stone fragments were dark, eroded, and covered with moss.

BY NOW WE HAD LOOKED at Paleokastritsa on Corfu's west coast and at the Kanoni peninsula on the east side of the island. Both were possible places where Odysseus had met with King Alcinous and Queen Arete before he left for Ithaca. We know that Odysseus landed on Corfu in a place where a river runs into the sea. Rivers are uncommon in Greece and even more so on the islands. It should be easy to locate the place.

According to Admiralty chart #206, Corfu has nine small rivers. Four are on the north coast, four are on the east coast, and one is to the west. The longest rivers (five miles) are in the north, but these are too remote from the ancient city sites that we investigated. The four on the east coast are either too seasonal or too remote. That leaves the Érmones river on the west coast, which runs from the Ropa valley west to the sea. The distance by road from Paleokastritsa to the mouth of the Érmones is about eight miles; to the Kanoni peninsula is seven miles. Both are within easy mule-cart range.

Since there were no buses to the Érmones river we rented a little car and drove west from Kérkira. The Érmones drains the inland Ropa valley, which runs northwest-southeast in the middle of the island for about four miles. The river then turns west and flows two miles to the sea. It was now the middle of summer and the river was low. Additionally we saw that some of the water had been diverted to farming. Nevertheless when we arrived at the sea we could

see a modest flow across the sandy beach and into the deep water of the ocean. The river carried a little soil with it and where the water ran into the sea the soil diffused and made a chocolate-colored stain in the blue sea. A large German hotel has been built high up on the north slope of the Érmones, and tall, blond children played on the beach below.

Was this the place where Odysseus swam ashore on that stormy night thirty-two centuries ago? Was this the stream where Nausicaa and her maids washed the clothing? Was this the meeting ground of the exhausted sailor and the welcoming young woman? As I've said before, Homer's tale is a story that I believe is based on mostly second-hand facts: a yarn that rests on a structure of real people and events. Corfu has a hundred arguments for being the home of the Phaeacians. A shipwrecked mariner could well have worked his way ashore in the little open bay of the Érmones. I think it makes sense.

But to answer the question: Was the ancient Phaeacian city at Paleokastritsa on the west side of Corfu or was it on the Kanoni peninsula on the east?

By the rules of evidence and by common sense, I have to say that the ancient city was on the Kanoni peninsula on the east side, perhaps under the forest of Mon Repos. But my heart tells me that the ancient city was on the west.

I think of the rocky spurs and cliffs, the sparkling blues of the

Where the river meets the sea: the mouth of the Ermones river. This is the place where Odysseus might have met Nausicaa. In the actual scene the silt from the river makes a big brown patch in the blue sea.

ocean, and the white accents of the breaking waves. Paleokastritsa has to be a place where the ancients settled and lived. It has beaches that are good for small fishing boats and easily fortified heights. A little inland are valleys fit for farming. There's timber for houses and boatbuilding—everything an enterprising group of people would have needed for a thriving settlement.

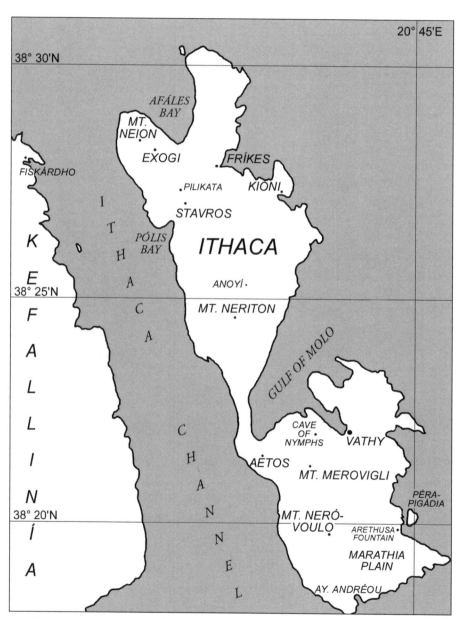

ITHACA

ITHACA
AT LAST

THE ADVANTAGE OF TRAVELING on a small yacht is that you take your bed, kitchen, and desk with you. You're in a sort of movable hotel. On board are all your requirements: a few favorite books, a protected cabin, lockers with food, tanks with drinking water, clothing, charts—everything you need.

But what about storms and gales? Pirates and thieves? Rolly anchorages? If you sail during the seasons of fine weather and pick your locations you can expect reasonable weather. Or said another way: the seasons of bad weather have been plotted and catalogued for a long time; by planning, it's possible to avoid severe storms—or most of them. You run into a gale now and then, but it's not the end of the world. Pirates and thieves? I have firsthand information about pirates who operate in the Sulu sea in the Philippines and in Phillip channel near Singapore. I don't sail there. Thieves? They're certainly around, but not many bother small yachts that anchor out. Most thieves don't know about boats; they don't have a small boat to come out to you, and if they did they'd be awkward and nervous. Ashore you might be mugged while you wait for a bus, but bus riders don't have much money. Thieves generally go after the wealthy. Rolly anchorages? They're a problem we try to avoid by picking those with good shelter.

A thirty-five-foot sailing yacht is a small home, which I find snug and satisfying. Of course compared with air travel, sea voyages are impossibly slow and pokey. Yet when you finally arrive at the other end, you have everything with you. Then you can linger in lovely places and explore rivers and estuaries. You can travel to islands that tourists never see and make friends with a thousand strangers if you wish. It's a nice way to see the world, but a pocket cruiser moves at the pace of a bicycle. You need to throw away the calendar.

IT WAS LATE JUNE when we sailed south from the city of Kérkira on the east coast of Corfu toward Port Vathi on Ithaca. The distance was only eighty-five miles, but it was the most exciting sail of our adventure because Ithaca was our last objective, our final goal. I felt that as I held the tiller in my hand and steered, I had a direct connection with the gods up on Mt. Olympus; certainly Zeus, Artemis, Athena, and all the rest would help us find our destination.

The wind was light, and it took us six hours to reach the south end of long, skinny Corfu. At Paleokastritsa we had noticed that fresh northwest winds often came up in the afternoon. Sure enough, as we cleared the tip of Corfu, the wind increased. We poled out a headsail and soon were tying reefs in the mainsail. A Dutch yacht about our size appeared, and we had an unofficial race, which was great fun for a couple of hours.

We stopped at the little island of Paxoí for the night because I wanted to arrive at Ithaca in daylight so we could have a good first look at the place. Paxoí's main harbor is tucked behind a small onshore islet. The shelter is excellent, and because of its isolation the little village is charming and quite unspoiled.

By noon the next day we had cleared Paxoí and were halfway to the southwest tip of Levkás. Again the northwest wind increased in the afternoon. By 1545 we had passed Levkás and with Kefallinía ahead, we changed course to the east-southeast to round Ithaca and head south along its eastern side. I was surprised at how large and high Kefallinía is and how it overshadows little Ithaca immediately to the east. Why, I wondered, wasn't Kefallinía the capital, and Ithaca the satellite island of Odysseus's ancient kingdom?

As we headed south and looked ahead we missed the trees of Corfu. We had crossed the rainfall line again because the steep

A view of the brown hills of Ithaca to the southeast from the tiny village of Fiskardo on Kefallinía, the high island to the west.

slopes of Kefallinía and Ithaca are barren except for scrub growth. Perhaps it's because Ithaca is twenty miles offshore and shielded from northerly winds by the island of Levkás. Other causes may be demon woodcutters of past centuries, the subsequent severe erosion of soil, less rainfall, and the lack of a conservation ethic.

Ithaca is thirteen miles long in a northwest-southeast direction. The mountainous island is three miles wide and consists of a north oval and a south oval connected by a craggy thread of land to the west. Immediately east of the connecting isthmus is the Gulf of Molo, which is two-and-a-half miles long and one mile wide. Port Vathi is a separate mile-long bay off the middle of the southern part of Molo. Port Vathi (which means deep port) is thus doubly protected from sea swell and storms. This wonderful natural harbor is one of the best in all of Greece for both large and small vessels. The place has an easy entry, moderate depths right up to the edges, and excellent holding ground for anchors. The only problem is that Vathi faces northwest and often receives fierce local afternoon winds that whistle down the entrance strait.

We skirted the east side of Ithaca and passed the small ports of Fríkes and Kióni. Late in the day we entered the Gulf of Molo. Since early morning we'd had fair winds; now in the shadow of

Vathy, the capital and main ferry terminal of Ithaca, from across the Gulf of Molo to the north.

Mt. Neriton we were becalmed. Far in the distance we could see a breeze brushing the water. Several fishing boats, an enormous high-sided blue ferry, and half a dozen yachts motored past us. I kept looking at the stark hills and mountains and tried to imagine Ithaca in ancient times. On the shoreline above the water I could see a rocky pathway. Who, I wondered, last walked on it?

An hour later the wind reached us. We turned to port and sailed to the southeast end of Port Vathi where we dropped a bow anchor and tied *Whisper's* stern to the central quay near the port captain's office. A narrow paved road ran around the edge of the bay. Immediately behind it were mostly two-story white houses with red tile roofs. Behind the first row of houses was a second row, and sometimes a third, all connected by narrow alleyways and whitewashed passages. The usual shops and cafés were nearby.

I had expected something a bit grander, but I learned that in 1953 a severe earthquake had devastated Vathi and toppled the fine Venetian buildings that dated from the sixteenth century. The islands of Ithaca, Levkás, and Kefallinía lie on a major earthquake fault. All have suffered crippling earthquakes in recent years, so the emphasis today is on low buildings of brick and reinforced concrete that are more shock resistant.[41]

But I wasn't concerned with earthquakes. I was thinking how pleased I was to be tied up in the main port of Ithaca. I could hardly believe it. After all the stops and months of sailing, we'd finally landed on the island where Homer ended his story. Were there any relics or hard evidence that this was the home of Odysseus? Did he actually exist? Are there significant Mycenaean ruins?

To begin with, let's quickly review the high spots of Homer's story after Odysseus returned to Ithaca. Then we can see if our present-day journey ties in with the ancient tale.

ODYSSEUS AND HIS VALUABLES were put ashore in Vathy, on the southwest side of the bay. Odysseus didn't recognize his island until the goddess Athena, who appeared disguised as a boy, told him where he was. Together they hid his treasure from Corfu in the nearby Cave of the Nymphs. Athena then disguised Odysseus as an old beggar and sent him to the south end of the island to see his old swineherd Eumaeus (yoo-ME-us).

As was the custom in the ancient world, Eumaeus welcomed the stranger and offered him food and lodging. The old beggar said he was from Crete and had seen Odysseus, who would soon return to Ithaca. Eumaeus, however, believed that both Odysseus and his son Telemachus (te-LEM-a-kus) were dead. The beggar stayed with Eumaeus.

Athena warned Telemachus (who was away on the mainland seeking his father) that the suitors planned to ambush and kill him. The suitors were a large group of young aristocrats, one of whom hoped to marry Penelope and take over Odysseus's role as king. Penelope stalled them off, weaving (by day) and un-weaving (by night) her famous tapestry, while she prayed that Odysseus would return. Meantime the suitors (all 108 of them) squandered the resources of the royal family by eating and drinking and having endless parties at the palace.

Telemachus managed to dodge the ambush ship sent out by the suitors. He landed on south Ithaca—probably at what is known today as Port St. Andrew. He then hurried to Eumaeus's hut and sent the old swineherd to the palace in the north to tell his mother that he was safe.

Odysseus, finally alone with Telemachus, told the young man that he was his father. Together they prepared to fight the suitors. Telemachus traveled to the palace. Later Odysseus, still disguised as a beggar, also walked to the palace. Once there, the suitors insulted and made fun of the old beggar until Penelope rebuked them.

To move weapons that might be used against them out of the way, Odysseus and Telemachus took the helmets, spears, and shields from the main hall and hid them in a storeroom. Later that evening, Penelope talked to the old beggar and confessed that her plan was to make the suitors wait until she had finished her weaving. When the suitors discovered that she was unraveling her work at night, however, they demanded that she immediately choose one of them for her new husband.

The beggar told Penelope that he was from Crete and that Odysseus—whom he described exactly—would return tomorrow. While washing his feet his old nurse Eurycleia (yoo-re-KLEYE-a) recognized him by a scar above one of his knees; he warned her to keep quiet. Finally and very reluctantly, Penelope agreed to wed the suitor who could string Odysseus's bow and shoot through the sockets of twelve axeheads lined up in a row.

Odysseus lay sleepless, listening to the weeping of Penelope, until Athena comforted him. Early the next morning the serving people prepared for the feast of Apollo. The suitors again thought of murdering Telemachus but were put off by bad omens.

Penelope brought out Odysseus's great bow and declared the trial open to the suitors. One after another tried to string the bow; no one could.

While the trials were going on, the old beggar took the swineherd Eumaeus and a friendly cowherd named Philoetius (fi-LEE-shus) outside and revealed to them that he was Odysseus, back home after twenty years. Both were overjoyed and promised help against the hated suitors.

More suitors tried to string the bow and failed. Then Odysseus asked to be allowed to try. The suitors scoffed, but Penelope insisted. Eumaeus handed him the bow; meanwhile Eurycleia fastened the door to the women's quarters. Philoetius sealed the exits from the hall.

Odysseus quickly strung his bow, took an arrow, and shot straight through the holes in the twelve axe-heads. Telemachus, fully armed, jumped up beside his father.

"Now for another target!" cried Odysseus, and with swift arrows from his bow he began to kill the suitors right and left. Soon his quiver was empty, and there was a great pile of bodies. Someone found weapons for twelve of the suitors, and they attacked with spears and swords. Soon it was the four on Odysseus's side vs. six well-armed suitors who hurled their razor-sharp spears as one to overwhelm the royalists. But with the help of Athena's magic the salvo missed the royal party and crashed into walls and doors. When the Odysseus Four threw *their* spears, however, they ran straight and true, and four more suitors died. Again four suitors flung deadly bronze spears; again Athena changed their courses to miss the Royalists. Back came four deadly lances, and four more suitors screamed and fell. Then came more hacking and stabbing and slashing. A severed head rolled in the blood and gore. The king and his men killed all the suitors except the bard and the herald who were declared innocent. Odysseus had the bodies removed, the hall cleaned up, and sulphur burned to purify the palace. The battle was over . . . it was finally over.

Eurycleia now brought a suspicious Penelope into the great

hall. She could not believe that the man before her was really Odysseus and refused to go to him. Odysseus said he'd sleep alone.

Penelope decided to test Odysseus and ordered Eurycleia to move the bed out of the sleeping room. "Spread it with blankets and fleeces to keep him warm," she said.

At that Odysseus grew angry and spoke up: "Now who could move my bed, which I built on a stump of olive."

When Penelope heard these words she knew the man in front of her was Odysseus because he had built the bedroom and constructed the bed on a stump of olive with his own hands. The words brought tears to her eyes; she ran to him, threw her arms around his neck, and kissed him again and again.

The relatives of the suitors banded together and planned revenge for the killings. A battle started, but Athena stopped the fighting and made peace. The story was over.

WAS ALL THIS A FAIRY TALE performed on Ithaca or did the story have some local basis in fact? We decided to look at everything to do with Odysseus.

The next morning we left *Whisper* lying to two anchors in Vathy bay and took the bus partway to Mt. Aetos (eagle). As we walked up on the low mountain we came to some ancient walls in an area known as Odysseus's castle. Who were the men, I wondered, who struggled to move these huge stones so long ago? The views, particularly of Kefallinía to the west and of the Ithaca channel below, were impressive. On the way back we passed a deserted archeological dig with a fence around it.

Since we were in the area we stopped at Dexia bay and took an alternate route to the Cave of the Nymphs. Dexia was tiny, only a quarter of a mile in diameter, and immediately west of Vathy bay.

It was a pretty place with a small beach and clumps of brush here and there. Yet it was directly exposed to the northwest and the strong afternoon wind and swell. A rough dirt road snaked up the valley south of the bay. It was a long, hot walk up a steep winding slope past abandoned currant grounds and farming fields. We were soon wringing wet.

Finally after a long switchback to the right we came to what seemed the end of the road and a sign that pointed uphill. We walked another fifty meters and came to the cave and its young Greek guardian. We paid a small admission fee and squeezed through the narrow entrance. As we entered the darkness we heard a generator cough into life; a dozen small electric bulbs revealed themselves and lighted our way.

The Cave of the Nymphs was the third cave we'd seen. The first was the Cave of Polyphemus at the west end of Sicily, a wide-mouthed cave that was long, open, and not very deep. It had a sheepfold at the entrance and a fine view of the sea. The second cave belonged to Calypso on Gozo. It was small and constricted with a difficult entrance. It had a good view of the sea from its mouth.

We found that Ithaca's Cave of the Nymphs had no view of the sea and was large and damp inside, with stalactites dotted around the ceiling and walls. Directly inside the entrance the floor was about two meters wide and ran back for six meters or so to a set of steps on the left. The steps led down to the main cavern, which was more or less circular and about eighteen meters in diameter. Overhead the roof was high and roughly spherical. At the extreme top was a small opening through which daylight poured in and which would have made a perfect ventilation hole for smoke from an inside warming fire during the winter.

The cave before us was surprisingly like Homer's description and serves to fix Odysseus's landing in the area. Again and again in this book I've suggested that Homer heard about these distant places from travelers and sailors. Yet how could he have known the intimate details he used in his account? The cave with two entrances, one for mortals and one for the gods. . . . The secrets of Homer are never-ending . . .

From the Cave of the Nymphs, Athena sent Odysseus, disguised as an old beggar, to find Eumaeus who lived on the plain of Marathia in the southeast part of Ithaca and who raised swine for the palace. To reach Marathia Margaret and I could have walked along an old trail from the Cave of the Nymphs. Instead we chose to sail from Port Vathy to the southeast coast near an islet called Péra Pigádi. We anchored *Whisper*, took the dinghy ashore, and walked up a steep path to Arethusa's spring. We had heard that this climb was a killer, but it was easy and took only twenty minutes.

I expected a great flowing spring because I had seen an 1821 A.D. painting of the spring, which showed trees, a double plunging waterfall, and people coming and going. Now the island is dry during the summer, and the output is almost nil. Nevertheless since we were there we put a cup under the spring and timed the flow at forty-two drops a minute. We were hot and thirsty. The water was clear and cold, and we drank it with gusto. A crude bucket arrangement existed at the spring; obviously there was plenty of water in other seasons.[42]

From near Arethusa's spring we could see the broad vertical cliff called Raven's crag. We saw some large birds, but they may have been hawks. Both places are mentioned in *The Odyssey*. Just above was the Marathia plateau where in ancient times Eumaeus had pigsties and his stone hut.

We walked up the trail to the plateau, a rocky area of small trees, shrubs, a little scratch cultivation, and sheep. Soon a neatly dressed man trotted by on a donkey on his way to a nearby house, paddock, and outbuildings. He was amazed at our presence and wanted to know where we'd come from. Margaret thumbed through her Greek dictionary and tried to ask about the trail to what is known today as Port St. Andrew (Ormos Ayios Andréou). The smiles were easy, but conversation was hopeless, and with a wave the man on the donkey disappeared. We saw another sheep-herder in rough garb and several primitive houses and sheds with stone walls and tin roofs. The fences were crude dry-wall construction topped with spiny shrubs.

We re-traced our steps down the steep slope to the little beach where we had left our dinghy, rowed out to *Whisper*, and sailed to the southern extremity of Ithaca. There we found Port St. Andrew (easier by sea than land). The place was a tiny slot in the mountains with excellent protection from all directions except

Man on donkey, Marathia plain.

south. We worked in close, dropped an anchor, and ran a stern line to the small rocky beach. We were alone and the place was utterly peaceful and quiet. The smell of thyme and sage drifted out to us; the only sound was the droning of cicadas. Was this the place, we wondered, where Telemachus landed on his way home from Nestor's palace at Pylos on the mainland after having been warned of an ambush by the suitors?

We took stock of our tour of the southern half of Ithaca. We had visited Mt. Aetos, the Cave of the Nymphs, and found the

Whisper *anchored in tiny Port St. Andrew.*

trail to the high land of Marathia. We had tasted water from the spring of Arethusa, photographed Raven's crag, and learned how people lived on the plateau. Except for wearing digital wrist watches and having better shoes, it seemed to us that the herders of today were not too far from what Homer talked about when he described Eumaeus.

Polis bay, Ithaca.

THE SEARCH
FOR THE PALACE

W E SAILED NORTH along the west side of Ithaca for another ten miles and anchored in Polis bay, which is notched into the mountains and almost surrounded by sharp-angled cliffs and slopes. The sun doesn't touch the waters of Polis until mid-morning and leaves early, so during the day the place is full of dramatic shadows and slanting sunbeams. To the west we looked across two miles of water to the bony mountains of Kefallinía. At the head of Polis bay is a small beach. Then a steep hill climbs up to the village of Stavrós, about a mile away.

But we were concerned with the north side of the bay and a rocky cliff that came down to the water. About 130 years ago the owner of the land found a small cave along the shore and dug up an ancient bronze tripod-cauldron. Later, in 1904, an investigator found pieces of Mycenaean pottery. In 1930-33, a British archeologist named Sylvia Benton and her assistants decided to make a thorough excavation of the site. However at some time in the past a mass of rocks had fallen from the ceiling of the cave at the entrance and covered part of the floor. The avalanche preserved the floor of the cave under the rocks from amateur prodding, but it also stopped the archeologists. The ingenious Miss Benton put on her miner's hat and supervised the blasting, breaking up, and removal of the rocks.

As Benton & Company dug they found that the floor of the cave had subsided since ancient times. When they reached depths

People buying fish, Polis bay.

of one meter or so they were flooded out because they were below sea level. Nevertheless the Greek workmen brought up pottery fragments and other items even though they labored in water up to their knees. The determined Miss Benton now put on her engineer's hat and with timbers and cement constructed two small dams across the entrance. After four attempts with small pumps she finally brought in a high-capacity pump from Patras to handle the water.

Miss Benton learned that the cave was in use from the early Bronze Age up to the first century A.D. However her most exciting finds were twelve bronze tripod-cauldrons, shards of Mycenaean pottery, and a small, triangular-shaped terracotta Hellenistic mask fragment from a religious offering with the Greek words: *A Prayer to Odysseus.*

The archeologists dated these relics about 800 B.C. This means they were contemporary with Homer and made about 400 years after Odysseus returned to Ithaca. Miss Benton concluded that she had found a small seaside shrine devoted to the memory and worship of Odysseus.[43]

After the work of Miss Benton the remnants of the cave collapsed during an earthquake. It's unclear when this happened, but today the site of the cave is only a pile of rocks. Miss Benton died in 1985 at the age of 94, but her work lives on in the small museum in Stavrós.

The next morning we rowed ashore to a small quay where a dozen fishermen were selling fish directly from their boats to the locals who lined up for a chance to buy. We toiled up the steep road to Stavrós where I saw a village square with a statue of Odysseus, a large empty church, a bakery, four tavernas, and a hardware store set among mostly white cement-block houses with red tile roofs. We soon found out that Stavrós, like the other villages on Ithaca, was steadily losing people. True, there were plenty of houses, but many of these had been closed for years because the owners had migrated to Australia, South Africa, or the U.S.

We walked to the little Stavrós museum, a nicely exhibited collection of valuables from the area. We met the curator, a bright-eyed Greek woman named Fotiní Couvaras, who was born in Johannesburg and spoke excellent English. She showed us large-handled earthen jars that once held oil or grain, ancient pots with three rings at the bottom (the mark of Ithaca), bronze spearheads, and fancy drinking vessels. Plus the famous bronze tripod-caldrons discovered by Miss Benton almost seventy years ago.

What exactly is a tripod-caldron? It's a circular cooking pot roughly 27 inches in diameter and 12 inches high supported by three legs two to four feet long. Sometimes the legs have small wheels so the contrivance can be rolled to or away from a fire. However a tripod-caldron was not only a simple cooking convenience or a way of heating water, but a Greek award or trophy for victory in boxing, running, chariot racing, or personal valor. A tripod-caldron was made to a high standard, carefully polished, and fitted with engraved handles, patterned edgings, and small raised figurines of horses, birds, and people. [44]

When Odysseus left Corfu he was presented with thirteen tripod-caldrons. Miss Benton found twelve in the cave and we know that one was dug up sixty years earlier. The dates don't add up and it may only be a coincidence of numbers, but it's an intriguing possibility that the tripod-caldrons in the Stavrós museum may be the originals from Corfu.

Mrs. Couvaras told us that while Miss Benton worked in the

Cave of the Tripods, another British archeologist, Professor W. A. Heurtley, attempted to find the location of the ancient Mycenaean city where Odysseus had his palace.

There are two possible sites. The first is on the southeast slope of Mt. Aetos on the narrow isthmus that connects the north and south halves of Ithaca. The Mt. Aetos area is above the sea and in a place well suited for defense and fortifications. The location is quite dramatic, and according to local legend it was the home of Odysseus's palace. After his excavations, however, Heurtley decided that the ruins he found were too recent to be connected with Homer. In addition he thought that Aetos didn't fit the descriptions in *The Odyssey*.

Heurtley moved to Pelikáta, the second site, in the north of the island. Pelikáta is a little north of Stavrós and in fact was not far from the little museum where we sat talking to Mrs. Couvaras.

"Pelikáta is on a little hill and has a wonderful view," she said. "From the site you can look into three harbors: Pólis to the southwest, Afáles to the north, and Fríkes to the east, all suitable for beaching the ancient ships, depending on the weather." [45]

We learned that Heurtley and his crew sank a series of trenches at Pelikáta and uncovered a significant Bronze Age site. The archeologists didn't find the remains of the ancient palace, but discovered Mycenaean artifacts and a large fortified wall. Heurtley decided that the building blocks used in later construction came from earlier Mycenaean buildings, perhaps from the palace itself. (Constructing the new from the old is common practice in modern Greece and Turkey.) Heurtley concluded that the site he uncovered was the most likely place for Odysseus's palace.

> "It is clear that those who think . . . that Pelikáta is the site of the palace of Odysseus can now support their case by respectable archaeological evidence," wrote Professor Heurtley in 1935. [46]

Now we fast forward almost two generations to 1984 when Dr. Sarantis Symeonoglou, an archeologist from Washington University in St. Louis, Missouri in the U.S., arrived in Ithaca to begin the first excavations in fifty years. Dr. Symeonoglou began to work at the ancient site on Mt. Aetos—up on the shoulder of the barren mountain at the south end of the narrow isthmus that joins the north and south parts of the island. Dr. Symeonoglou decided to expand the work of the British in the 1930s, and he put together a group of associates, students, volunteers, and local workmen.

During fourteen summers of digging on a difficult, eroded site, the present-day excavators uncovered the ruins of a sizeable settlement. The ancient town existed on the saddle below Mt. Aetos from 1400 B.C. all the way to the first century B.C. when the people moved to Vathy. This means that the city was active from the era of the Trojan War through the time of Homer. The evidence of the city, which might have been called Ithaca (like the island), is based on ancient private and public buildings, towers, gates, a cistern, and numerous local bronze coins (some of which show Odysseus). There are fortifications, a road, thousands of potsherds from many eras, a pottery shop, stone pavements, and both a temple and an outdoor shrine to Apollo.

In 1992, to take one example, the archeologists in the Odyssey Project, as it is called, moved hundreds of large rocks, dug down 4.5 meters, and exposed a Mycenaean building 22–25 meters long. A stone dome had once covered part of the building, which was constructed in 1300 B.C. By using well-established dating techniques and other evidence, the archeologists learned that the stone dome stood for a thousand years until it collapsed in the fourth century, probably from an earthquake. Dr. Symeonoglou believes the structure was a fountain or cistern used to store water during the rainy season for use during the dry summer. This structure may be the one mentioned in chapter 17 of *The Odyssey*:

> And when, as they went on along the rugged path,
> They got near the city, they arrived at a spring,
> Paved and fair-flowing, whence the townswomen drew water,
> Which Ithakos, Neritos, and Polyktor had made.
> About it was a grove of poplars nourished by water
> In a circle on all sides, and cold water flowed down
> From the rock above. An altar had been built above
> To the nymphs, where all travelers made offerings. [47]

VIEW OF MT. AETOS LOOKING WEST

Since the early 1980s, Dr. Sarantis Symeonoglou, an archeologist from Washington University in St. Louis, Missouri USA, has concentrated his summer field work at Mt. Aetos on Ithaca. He has made many significant discoveries, but probably the most important is that the site is far more complex and difficult to work than anyone suspected. Like all scientists who quest for the ultimate truth, Dr. Symeonoglou hopes for The Big Find. On Ithaca this is the Palace of Odysseus. Each summer the learned doctor comes to Ithaca with 20–24 students, assistants, and workmen to pursue his excavations and studies. For a sample of his work, here is a photograph of Mt. Aetos with numbers and corresponding explanations by Dr. Symeonoglou.

1. Site of the Homeric city of Ithaka on the east slope of Mt. Aetos. Here our team discovered ancient remains dating back to the 13th century B.C. The site was continuously inhabited until the time of Christ. We believe that the palace of Odysseus is somewhere on this slope, and we hope to excavate whatever remains of it. Our work is made difficult by the huge quantity of rocks used to build the terracing walls seen in the photo.

2. Citadel of the Classical city of Alalkomenai, circled by fortifications resembling Cyclopean construction and mistaken in the past as Mycenaean (the locals called it "the Castle Of Ulysses"). Following the construction of these fortifications (probably after 427 B.C.), the name of the city was changed from Ithaka to Alalkomenai. In the past, some scholars searched for two different cities in separate locations.

3. Easternmost extension of Alalkomenai, on the slopes of Mt. Merovigli (Homeric Neion). Our excavations revealed remains from the 4th–1st centuries B.C.

4. Fortifications encircling the lower citadel of Classical Alalkomenai. In this area, we located many houses and an ancient road leading to the top of Mt. Aetos.

5. Site of the British excavations of the 1930s, next to the chapel of St. George, now in ruins. Here we found an outdoor shrine with

View of Mt. Aetos looking west

many offerings. We believe that the shrine, dating from the 9th-6th centuries B.C., was dedicated to the cult of Apollo, mentioned by Homer in *The Odyssey*.

6. In 1986 we identified a large building, originally thought to be a tower, as a temple. We believe it was the temple of Apollo, built ca. 500 B.C. to replace the outdoor shrine nearby (no. 5).

7. In 1985 we excavated a house of the Geometric period (8th century B.C.) that was the first solid clue of the city that Homer saw.

8. Site of the 1986 excavations. We found several houses, two public buildings, a burial site, and, for the first time, pottery dating to the Mycenaean period. The center of the ancient city extends between points 7 and 8.

9. In 1985 our team excavated a rich house, destroyed ca. 300 B.C. It yielded the richest find on the island so far, a hoard of twenty-eight coins.

10. The ancient cemetery begins here and extends north toward the sea.

Earlier, two of the members of the Odyssey Project had taken aerial photographs that showed a large circle around the fountain. The poplars were long gone, but experts on the ground found a circular wall that had collapsed toward the center. As the digging continued, the team discovered the skeleton of a cow or bull—burned and with cut marks—and dozens of offerings—vases, bronzes, ivories, and amber. Every clue in *The Odyssey* was confirmed.

Dr. Symeonoglou and his team are still hard at work and hope to find the crown jewel of Odysseus's world: his palace. They're also seeking a theater, a sports stadium, and inscriptions that will finally settle all the Ithaca questions. If this ancient city truly emerges from the past, it could become one of the major archeological attractions of Greece. Unfortunately Dr. Symeonoglou is obliged to spend much of his time raising money to support his expedition. [48]

With respect to the work of Heurtley, Symeonoglou, and others, there's a great deal of talk about the palace of Odysseus and his nearby city. But these terms could be much exaggerated. True, Odysseus was a king, and kings rule from palaces. But the kingdom of Ithaca seems a modest operation. When Telemachus traveled to Pylos and entered a real palace he was stunned at its grandeur. This suggests that Odysseus's palace was more a local headquarters for a ruling magistrate. Similarly, the city may have been a modest town. Again in *The Iliad* when Odysseus tried for Helen's hand in competition with a dozen other young princes, he felt himself quite outclassed and instead wound up asking for Penelope. Perhaps archeologists digging on Ithaca may be looking for too much.

Since the years of Heurtley and Miss Benton, many researchers have taken up the hunt for the famous palace. As we have seen, Professor Symeonoglou is working (1998) at Mt. Aetos. Meanwhile Dr. A. Papadopoulos and a team from the University of Ioannina in western Greece are investigating sites near Stavrós. There's plenty of new material, but the stories are complicated and unclear because of the ancient, overlapping ruins and the severe soil erosion on Ithaca. In many ways the work must be like sorting old film negatives. Most are faded and give the viewer a clue only now and then. Who knows whether the story will ever be finalized.

Soil erosion is a constant factor in trying to explain the past in the Mediterranean islands. In his book *The Quest for Ulysses*, Professor J. V. Luce has a photograph (p. 88) of an ancient stone coffin cut into a large rock in the Late Bronze Age. At that time the soil must have covered the rock, which now is four or five feet above the ground. Certainly few people can travel among the Greek and Italian islands without wondering where the forests and soil have gone.

A few people who have written about Ithaca speak of controversy between proponents of the excavations in Aetos and the archeologists who have worked in Pelikáta. However I see the quest for the story of the ancient days as a search for the truth. Whether Odysseus belongs to Aetos or Pelikáta or somewhere else is not important. The main thing is to learn about our ancestors. Scholars sometimes claim too much for their work or belittle the efforts of others. I think Ithaca should not be a land to be disputed about, but a place to be savored and relished, an island where the nearby fingers of the sea remind us that *The Odyssey* is the story of a sailor. The book was written not to be pulled and pushed, but to be enjoyed. [49]

Margaret and I walked north to Pelikáta, a site we thought was a reasonable place for Odysseus's headquarters and settlement. There was a cooling breeze from the northwest, and from the top of the slight rise we could see for miles in all directions. If pirates had come to attack the palace, the hill and fortified wall would have helped in the defense of the place. If Odysseus, the self-proclaimed great warrior, wanted to overpower a passing trading ship or take part of her cargo as tribute it would have been easy to supervise an attack from these heights. There are good springs nearby, and a little to the north—just east of the village of Exogí— is an excellent area for farming and raising fruit and nut trees. We looked down at the three harbors: Polis toward Kefallinía, Afáles toward Levkás, and Fríkes toward the mainland.

The verses of Homer have clues that seem to relate to this neighborhood, and we wondered if we were tramping over the stones of the palace. Perhaps here was where Penelope had her upstairs room. Maybe over there was the great hall where the suitors gorged themselves on beef and pork, drank red wine, told jokes, and listened to the minstrel play his lyre. Here was the place where the old beggar had strung his mighty bow and with his son and loyal slaves had killed the usurpers.

The modern Pelikáta in front of us was cluttered with piles of rubble and marred by the construction of new summer villas erected by wealthy Greeks from Athens. Were the Greeks wasting the heritage of Homer by failing to make Pelikáta and the dramatic site on Mt. Aetos national archeological parks? Should the Greek government subsidize the excavations, build museums, and perhaps consider limited restorations? Should the Greeks promote their most famous author with festivals and summer concerts? Should they work to attract thousands of visitors to this desperately poor island? If this happened, could the politicians be induced to keep their hands out of the funds for the archeologists, conservators, and museum directors?

But who am I, a mere visitor from afar, to ask such questions?

WE RETURNED TO *Whisper* in Polis bay. A few days later when the wind was suitable we sailed around to the tiny ports of Fríkes and Kióni. The next morning we took a bus trip around the northern part of the island. We now had been in all the villages and learned that the present official population figure for Ithaca is 3,648. (In 1880 the population was 13,000.)

On inquiry, I was told that Vathi had 1,715 year-round residents, down from 2,037. Stavrós had 310. Anoyí, a small place on the north slope of Mt. Neriton, had 70. Fríkes with 40, was almost asleep. Exogí, also with 40 (once 2,000), was hardly breathing. In some places I saw houses but no people. When I began to look closely at the buildings I realized that many were shut up. The locks on the doors were rusty, and the shrubs were dead. Abandoned houses were dotted all over the landscape. Kióni, which in recent years had 400 families, was down to 210 people, and when I walked around I saw large trees growing inside roofless houses. We discovered that in 1960 the Kióni school had an enrollment of 65 pupils; today there are only two students.

The five villages in the north add up to 670 people. Together with Vathi the total is 2,385. I added another five percent for isolated families. This gives 2,504, but this figure is only 69 percent of the official population figure for Ithaca. There are some children, of course, but far too many residents have gray hair and live on retirement checks from abroad.[50]

The island exports a little olive oil, red wine, and currants, but the tannery is closed. Other earnings come from tourism and modest fishing. There's no airport, only a single bus, and two small hotels.

It doesn't take much reasoning to point out that if these trends continue, Ithaca will soon have no people at all. Has the place merely become a summertime colony for tourists? Will present-day Ithaca fade away like the palace of Odysseus?*

We added up what we'd seen in the northern half of Ithaca. The fact that we'd been in Polis (which means city) bay was a clue in itself to the location of an ancient settlement. We had visited the ruined Cave of the Tripods and examined dozens of local artifacts in the museum. So many details of Ithaca check out with *The Odyssey* that it's hard to ignore the notion that Homer must have visited Ithaca in person before he put his story together.

Setting aside the obvious bits of fantasy in *The Odyssey*, I believe the story is true. Homer was a genius in bringing to life a motley collection of good and bad people within the framework of a vanished civilization. Odysseus is unforgettable because like all men he's strong and weak, clever and foolish, a tough guy and a coward. He disgusts us with his braggadocio one minute and then turns around and charms us with his ingenuity the next. Whenever Homer's plot wavers he fills in the blanks by using a sky full of superior gods whose magic creates/solves all problems in the world below. But to keep things from glowing too much he employs a nether world of the pitiful dead to balance his story.

Did Homer invent his world? I doubt it. According to the Columbia Encyclopedia, Fifth Edition, 1993, p. 1,868:

> The works of Homer have been radically reevaluated since the archaeological discoveries of Mycenaean Greece. He is now considered to give admirable glimpses of the culture of the late Mycenaean civilization of the 12th cent. B.C.

---

*Or to take the problem one step further: What is the future of the small Greek islands? But that's another story.

*Vase with dancing figures. By the artist Nikosthenes,
c. 535 B.C.*

If you've read this far, you know that Margaret and I sailed
first to Troy. Then south through the Aegean and past Cape
Malea to southern Tunisia. Next we headed to the west coast of
Sicily, the southern tip of Corsica, and the west coast of Italy.
Then south to the Strait of Messina, to Malta, and northeast to
Corfu. Finally we skipped south to Ithaca where the voyages
ended.

We visited nineteen places—some real, some will-o-the-
wisps—where Odysseus might have stopped. We based our itinerary on common-sense sailing, lots of reading, and an appreciation
of Homer. Because of the weather and seasons this took two years.
We thought we made a fairly quick and thorough tour of all the
sites, considering the widespread locations. Certainly the experi-

ence of sailing from one place to the next gave us a felicitous grasp of Homer's story.

Our route following Odysseus totaled 2,650 nautical miles. However from Troy to our last visit to the west coast of Sicily we logged 6,500 miles or 2.45 times as much. We sailed up and down the Turkish coast looking for clues about Odysseus. We visited Crete, the Eolie islands, and the peninsulas of northern Sardinia. Several times we turned around and sailed back to yesterday's port because I had a new idea for a photograph. On our way from Cape Circeo to Scilla, Margaret pointed out that we'd somehow missed the Galli islands, so we turned back to look for the Sirens. We went round the Pelopónnisos four times, made two trips to the museums in Athens, and returned to Míkonos a second time to photograph an ancient vase with a drawing of the Trojan horse.

We followed a lot of blind leads and false hopes and tried to refine our voyage of fantasy into something we trust Homer would have approved. What tied our story together were the sea and the sailing and the islands and the anchorages and the ordinary people we met.

The most enjoyable places for me were the remote islands and coastlines that were cut off from air travel. Places where olive oil was sold by the dipperful, where you traded a hose clamp for a fish, where you bought a live chicken, where peasant women gave you smiles and fresh flowers, and where traveling meant hiking or riding on a donkey. It was all a wonderful experience and one I'd be glad to repeat. But I've already had the pleasure a second time while I wrote the pages of this book.

In the end the modern Greek poet Constantine Cavafy (1863–1933) may have said it best of all:

Be sure you are quite old when you drop anchor in Ithaca.

Rich with the experience you have gained upon your voyage.

Do not expect the island to give you riches

Ithaca has given you your wonderful voyage.

NOTES

1. For biographies of Schliemann, the bizarre but enterprising archeologist, see Payne, *Gold of Troy*, and Moorehead, *Lost Treasures*. Deuel, *Memoirs of Schliemann*, has a good introduction and excerpts from Schliemann's unsteady writings.

2. The best book on early warships I've found is Casson, *The Ancient Mariners*, chapter 3. Casson also has some apt comments on the Greek character on pp. 35–36. For an idea of a Bronze Age cargo ship of 32 centuries ago, see Bass, *Archaeology*.

3. For early population figures, see Casson, *Ancient Mariners*, p. 113. Others dispute Casson's figures and claim that Athens had a maximum population of 100,000 in ancient times.

4. Tuchman, *March of Folly*, p. 36.

5. Many books and relics in Greek museums attest to the grandeur of the Mycenaean world. See Casson, *Ancient Mariners*, p. 26; MacKendrick, *The Greek Stones Speak*, pp. 58–152; Stanford & Luce, *The Quest for Ulysses*, chap. 3; and Papahatzis, *Mycenae-Epidaurus-Tiryns-Nauplion*. The color drawings of Piet de Jong in *Homer and the Heroic Age*, by J. V. Luce, p. 82, though based to some extent on conjecture, give a good idea of Nestor's palace.

6. For remarks on Homer's technique and style, see the preface (pp. xxxiii to xlviii, by Walter James Miller) in the Butler translation of *The Odyssey* in the Simon & Schuster paperback.

7. Encyclopaedia Britannica, 11th ed., s.v. "Homer" p. 689.

8. For comments on modern Yugoslavian storytellers and their parallel with ancient Greek bards, see Parry, *Homeric Verse*.

9. Fagles, *Iliad*, Book 17, lines 48–56. p. 444.

10. The story of the letter illustrates the inconsistencies in trying to deal with this material. According to some authorities, writing was a marginal skill that may or may not have been known to Homer. Paper and parchment belonged to the future. No one seems to be certain whether papyrus or other writing material was available in the eastern Aegean in 750 B.C. If it were, writing was at a rudimentary level. We know that clay tablets were used in Cnossus in 1400 and in Pylos in 1200, but only for routine inventories. How then could Odysseus have planted the forged letter in Palamedes's tent during the Trojan War which took place in 1200 B.C., 450 years earlier? The Palamedes story is from *Cypria*, an epic poem that described the situation prior to the Trojan War. See Stanford & Luce, *The Quest for Ulysses*, p. 16, and Bérard, *Did Homer Live?* pp. 17–28; 60–61. Also Andrewes, *The Greeks*, p. 23. A similar problem is iron vs. bronze. Homer's heroes use bronze weapons (not usual in Homer's time), and workmen use iron tools (not possible in the Bronze Age). See Johnston, *Emergence of Greece*, p. 50

11. For details of Ismarus and Maróneia and a useful map, see Bakirtzis and Trianataphyllos, *Thrace*, pp. 50–58.

12. Bass, *Archaeology.*

13. Doumas. *The Wall Paintings of Thera.* pp. 68–83. A stunning book in color of the recently discovered (1974) frescoes in an ancient Greek village. The paintings were preserved under tons of volcanic ash for 36 centuries. One painting shows Greek ships 428 years before the Trojan War. Many of these restored frescoes are on display in a special room in the National Archaeological Museum in Athens. The paintings on view are a miracle of patience and advanced restoration techniques.

14. Casson, *Ancient Mariners*, p. 36.

15. Lawrence, T. E., *Odyssey*, book 9, p. 92. Lawrence's fine prose translation was first published in 1932. Lawrence, nobody's fool, thought that Odysseus was a "cold-blooded egotist."

16. The palm tree material is from Lawrence, book 6, p. 68; Concerning Delos, see Bradford, *Greek Islands*, pp. 120–128; Ludwig, *Mediterranean*, p. 72; MacKendrick, *Greek Stones*, various entries; Zaphiropoulou, *Delos*, pp. 5–11.

17. Denham, *Ionian Islands to Rhodes*, pp. 76–77. Captain Denham's excellent sailing directions in his various guides are first-rate. Even though dated they should be carried on every small vessel. Charming drawings.

18. Rieu, *Odyssey*, book 9, p. 141.

19. Admiralty Pilot, *The Mediterranean*, vol. 1 and 5. The British Pilots are of inestimable value to sailors.

20. Zaphiropoulou, *Delos*, pp. 5–24.

21. Zaphiropoulou, *Delos*, p. 17.

22. Rieu, *Odyssey*, book 9, p. 141.

23. Herodotus, *Persian Wars*, p. 362.

24. An exhaustive summary of a hundred or more authors who have investigated Homer is in Hyde, *Ancient Mariners*, chapter 4.

25. For sailing without a compass, see Lewis, *We, the Navigators*.

26. Rieu, *Odyssey*, book 9, pp. 143–144.

27. For an excellent article on the Ègadis see Theresa M. Magi, "Ancient Islands in the Sun," *New York Times*, July 9, 1995; Denham, *Tyrrhenian Sea*, 126–129 & 71–73. Denham explains the ancient communal method of netting giant tuna.

28. I thought I was so clever in suggesting that Marettimo was a more sensible choice only to find out recently that P. Champault wrote about this almost a century ago. *Phéniciens et Grecs en Italie d'après l'Odyssée*, Paris, 1906.

29. Butler, *The Authoress of the Odyssey*, p. 194. Butler, a keen scholar of Homer, was greatly taken with a drawing of a young woman found on a piece of slate and believed to be from the Christian era of Greece. The drawing is in the museum at Cortona and is supposed to be of Nausicaa. According to Butler, most of the action in *The Odyssey* took place around the big island of Sicily. Butler believed that a woman wrote *The Odyssey*, and he sets forth many ingenious and clever arguments. Also see Graves, Robert. *Homer's Daughter*, New York: Doubleday, 1955. Some enterprising lady author of today ought to take a whack at this subject.

30. Bradford, *Ulysses Found*, pp. 77–88. A scholarly book with limited emphasis on following the route by yacht. Bradford, a popular historian, who lived in Malta and wrote a dozen excellent books about the Mediterranean, died in 1986.

31. Bérard, *Did Homer Live?* pp. 139–167. Bérard, a French intellectual and philologist, spent his life writing a shelf of stimulating and original books about Odysseus.

32. Bérard, pp. 131–134. Additionally, Dr. S. Symeonoglou has written me as follows (12-20-98): "You should know also that until 750 B.C. there was no writing, so the old stories about Italy (some going back to 1700 B.C.) were transmitted orally and were priceless."

33. Homer, *Odyssey*, Pope translation, pp. 442–443.

34. Bérard, pp. 155–156.

35. Denham, *Tyrrhenian Sea*, pp. 105–108; Heikell, *Italian Waters Pilot*, pp. 290–291.

36. Admiralty Pilot, *The Mediterranian*, vol. 1, 1978, pp. 226–227.

37. Admiralty Pilot for 1854, *The Mediterranean*. See note under Smyth in bibliography.

38. Fagles, *Odyssey*, book 5, p. 159. A 1996 translation that includes an introduction by Bernard Knox and a pronouncing glossary for difficult Greek names.

39. Stanford & Luce, *Quest for Ulysses*, photograph 98 & caption; The information about Durrell comes from an old (1950?) very poor CBS film titled: "The Search for Ulysses." Available from Carousel Videos, 260 Fifth Ave. NY 10001; Durrell, Greek Islands, p. 24. Also see an essay by Michel Gall in Lessing, *Voyages*, pp. 32–33.

40. Tataki, *Corfu*, pp. 41–44; Bradford, *Ulysses Found*, pp. 204–206; Bradford, *Greek Islands*, pp. 34–37.

41. Schildt, *In the Wake of Ulysses*, pp. 97–101; Bradford, *Greek Islands*, pp. 48–52; Denham, *Ionian Islands*, pp. 30–33, photos p. 45; An excerpt from Schliemann's visit in 1868 is in Lessing, *Voyages*, pp. 15–38; See Stanford & Luce, *Quest*, for chapter and map on Ithaca. Also Luce, *Homer and the Heroic Age*, pp. 140–155; Grosvenor, M. B. "Homeward with Ulysses to the Ionian Isles of Greece." National Geographic, July 1973.

42. The painting "The Fountain of Arethusa, after Jos. Cartwright in Views Dedicated to T. Maitland" is in Stanford & Luce, *Quest*, p. 102.

43. Lord Rennell, "The Ithaca of the Odyssey," *Annual of the British School at Athens*, vol. 33 (1933), pp. 16–19. Also Sylvia Benton "Excavations in Ithaca 3, The Cave at Polis," *Annual*, vol. 35 (1935): pp. 45–73.

44. Benton, "Evolution of the Tripod-Lebes," *Annual*, vol. 35 (1935): pp. 74–130.

45. Homer implies that two harbors are visible from the palace site. See Luce, *Quest*, p. 97. This is true only if you agree that Polis bay is "our" bay and that Reithron cove is present-day Frikes bay. This is likely, but not everyone agrees that Homer actually says this.

46. W. A. Heurtley, "Excavations in Ithaca 2," *Annual*, vol. 35: p. 44.

47. Albert Cook, *The Odyssey*, book 17, lines 204–211.

48. Dr. Sarantis Symeonoglou, "The Ithaca Question," *Greece Travel Magazine*, Jan/Feb. 1997, pp. 62–73. See also issues of *The Siren* for 1985–89, 90–91, & 92–93. For information about his work, The Odyssey Project, and fund-raising, see http://www.artsci.wustl.edu/~ssymeono/summary.html

49. Part of this argument is paraphrased from Ernle Bradford, *Greek Isles*, p. 52.

50. Figures collected by the author in 1997. The 1998 total population figure is taken from the web site of the Greek tourist bureau. The 1880 figure is from the British Admiralty Pilot for 1880 (p. 310).

BIBLIOGRAPHY

Books marked with an asterisk* were especially helpful.

* Admiralty Sailing Directions. *The Mediterranean*, vols. 1 through 5. Hydrographer of the Navy. Various dates after 1978.

Andrewes, Antony. *The Greeks*. New York: Norton, 1967.

* Bakirtzis, Ch. and Triantaphyllos, D. *Thrace*. Athens: The ETBA Cultural Foundation & Greek National Tourism Org., 1990.

Bass, George F. *Archaeology Beneath the Sea*. New York: Walker, 1975.

* Bérard, Victor. *Did Homer Live?* Translated by Brian Rhys. New York: E. P. Dutton, 1931.

Bowra, C. M. *Classical Greece*. New York: Time, Inc. 1965.

* Butler, Samuel. *The Authoress of the Odyssey*. New York: Longmans, Green. 1897.

* Bradford, Ernle. *The Wind Off the Island*. London: Hutchinson, 1960. A lovely book about a year-long sailing trip around Sicily in the 1950s.

* Bradford, Ernle. *The Companion Guide to The Greek Islands*. New York: Harper & Row, 1963.

* Bradford, Ernle. *Ulysses Found*. London: Hodder and Stoughton, 1963.

Brandon, Robin. *South France Pilot*. Huntingdon, Cambridgeshire: Imray, Laurie, Norie & Wilson, 1983. Chapter VI on Corsica.

* Casson, Lionel. *The Ancient Mariners*. New York: Macmillan, 1959.

* Denham, H. M. *The Ionian Islands to Rhodes, a sea-guide*. New York: W. W. Norton, 1972.

* Denham, H. M. *The Tyrrhenian Sea, A Sea-Guide to its Coasts and Islands*. New York: W. W. Norton, 1969.

* Denham, H. M. *The Aegean, A Sea-Guide to its Coasts and Islands*. London: John Murray, First published in 1963 and updated five times.

* Deuel, Leo. *Memoirs of Heinrich Schliemann*. New York: Harper & Row, 1977.

Doika, Kosta. *The Big Secret of Homer*. Athens: Edition Dodoni, 1993.

* Doumas, Christos. *The Wall Paintings of Thera*. Translated by Alex Doumas. Athens: The Thera Foundation and Petros M. Nomikos, 1992.

Durrell, Lawrence. *The Greek Islands*. New York: Viking Press, 1978.

Eliot, Alexander. *Greece*. New York: Time Inc. 1963.

* Finley, M. I. *The World of Odysseus*. New York: Penguin, 1954.

* Finley, M. I. *The Ancient Greeks*. New York: Viking, 1963.

* Gage, Elent N., editor. *Let's Go*. New York: St. Martin's Press, 1995. The Budget Guide to Greece & Turkey. A well-written, extremely useful guidebook. Buy the latest number.

Goldsmith, Capt. M. L. "Rame's Cruise Among the Ionian Islands." The Royal Cruising Club Journal for 1927.

Grant, Michael and Pottinger, Don. *Greeks*. Edinburgh: Thomas Nelson, 1958.

Graves, Robert. *The Siege and Fall of Troy*. New York: Dell, 1962.

Graves, Robert. *Greek Myths*. Illustrated Edition. London: Penguin, 1955.

Halliburton, Richard. *The Glorious Adventure*. Garden City, New York: Bobbs-Merrill, 1927.

Hamilton, Edith. *The Greek Way*. New York: W. W. Norton, 1930.

* Heikell, Rod. *Greek Waters Pilot*. St. Ives, Huntingdon, Cambridgeshire: Imray, Laurie, Norie & Wilson, 1985.

* Heikell, Rod. *Italian Waters Pilot*. St. Ives, Cambridgeshire: Imray, Laurie, Norie & Wilson, 1991.

* Heikell, Rod. *Turkish Waters Pilot*. Huntingdon, Cambridgeshire: Imray, Laurie, Norie & Wilson, 1985.

Herodotus. *The Persian Wars*. Translated by George Rawlinson. New York: Modern Library, 1947, p. 362.

* Homer. *The Odyssey*. Translated by Robert Fagles. New York: Viking, 1996.

* Homer. *The Odyssey*. Translated by Richard Latimore. New York: HarperCollins, 1967.

* Homer. *The Odyssey*. Translated by T. E. Lawrence. Ware, Hertfordshire: Wordsworth, 1992.

* Homer. *The Odyssey*. Translated by E. V. Rieu. New York: Penguin, 1946.

Homer. *The Odyssey*. Translated by Alexander Pope. New Haven: Yale University Press, 1967. The translation of 1725–26.

Homer. *The Odyssey.* Translated by Samuel Butler. Revised by Malcolm M. Willcock. New York: Simon & Schuster, Pocket Books, 1969.

Homer. *The Odyssey.* Translated by Albert Cook. New York: W. W. Norton, 1967.

* Homer. *The Iliad.* Translated by Martin Hammond. New York: Penguin, 1987. Unlike other translations of Homer, this paperback has an index, of inestimable value in sorting out the characters and action.

* Homer. *The Iliad.* Translated by Robert Fagles. New York: Viking, 1990.

* Hyde, Walter Woodburn. *Ancient Greek Mariners.* New York: Oxford University Press. 1947.

Innes, Hammond. *Sea and Islands.* New York: Knopf, 1967.

* Johnston, Alan. *The Emergence of Greece.* New York: E. P. Dutton, Elsevier Phaidon, 1976. Wonderful text and color photographs.

Kazantzakis, Nikos. *The Odyssey.* Translated by Kimon Friar. New York: Simon and Schuster, 1958. A modern epic poem. Great stuff, but fairly hard going.

Kerényi, C. *The Heroes of the Greeks.* London: Thames and Hudson, 1974.

Kokkinou, Sophia. *Greek Mythology.* Athens: Intercarta, 1989.

* Lessing, Erich. *The Voyages of Ulysses.* Basle: Herder Freiburg, 1965.

Lewis, David. *We, the Navigators.* Honolulu: University Press of Hawaii, 1972.

Loomis, Alfred F. *Hotspurs's Cruise in the Aegean.* New York: Jonathan Cape & Harrison Smith. 1931.

* Luce, J. V. *Homer and the Heroic Age.* New York: Harper & Row, 1975.

Ludwig, Emil. *The Mediterranean, Saga of a Sea.* New York: McGraw-Hill, Whittlesey House, 1942.

* MacKendrick, Paul. *The Greek Stones Speak.* New York: St Martin's, 1962.

McEvedy, Colin. *The Penguin Atlas of Ancient History.* Harmondsworth: Penguin, 1967.

Moorehead, Caroline. *The Lost Treasures of Troy.* London: Weidenfeld & Nicholson, 1994. Schliemann biography.

Obregon, Mauricio. *Ulysses Airborne.* New York: Harper & Row, 1971. A clever author, but dreary photographs.

Pagine Azzurre (Blue Pages). Guida Internazionale al diporto nautico (International guide for nautical sports). Rome: Pagine Azzurre, 1996. A large-format guide to the coastlines of Italy. In Italian, but still useful for non-Italian readers.

Papahatzis, Nicos. *Mycenae-Epidaurus-Tiryns-Nauplion.* Athens: Clio, 1986. A local guidebook.

Parry, Milman. *The Making of Homeric Verse.* New York: Oxford University, 1971.

Payne, Robert. *The Gold of Troy.* New York: Funk & Wagnalls, 1959. A good short biography of Schliemann.

* Schildt, Göran. *In the Wake of Ulysses.* Translated by Alan Blair. London: The Travel Book Club, 1953. A 1951 cruise through Greece in a 34-foot ketch by a Swedish couple.

* Schoder, Raymond V. *Wings Over Hellas. Ancient Greece from the Air.* New York: Oxford University, 1974. A series of 140 excellent color photographs, with 138 clever diagrams and authoritative captions. Handy and informative. The author, a Jesuit priest, used a financial grant to reduce the retail price of the book, a laudable move.

Severin, Tim. *The Ulysses Voyage.* New York: E. P. Dutton, 1987.

Smyth, William Henry. *The Mediterranean.* London: John Parker, 1854, p. 181. An early Admiralty pilot, commercially printed but often shelved with the modern Admiralty pilot books under 'Hydrographic Office.'

* Stanford, W. B. and Luce, J. V. *The Quest for Ulysses.* New York: Praeger, 1974. Ulysses from Homer to James Joyce, including much art work.

Tataki, A. B. *Corfu. Athens*: Ekdotike Athenon, 1979. A local guidebook.

Tuchman, Barbara W. *The March of Folly. From Troy to Vietnam.* New York: Alfred Knopf, 1984.

Zaphiropoulou, Photini, *Delos.* Athens: Krene, 1993.

INDEX

INDEX

ABOUT THE AUTHOR

HAL ROTH, born in 1927, was raised in Cleveland, Ohio. He was a flier during World War II and the Korean War, and graduated from the University of California in 1952 with a degree in journalism. He studied photography with Ansel Adams and Edward Weston, and worked as a free-lance magazine writer and photographer for many publications including *Collier's, Fortune, The Saturday Evening Post*, and *The New York Times*.

While writing a story in Yosemite Park for *Sunset* magazine, he became intrigued with the Sierra Nevada and made many trips to the high mountains. This led to his first book, *Pathway in the Sky* (1965), a words-and-picture story about the John Muir Trail.

In 1962, Roth and his wife, Margaret, went sailing on a friend's ketch in San Francisco Bay. Neither knew anything about sailing, but they liked it. They chartered yachts (with captains) in Greece and the Caribbean and learned to sail. Meanwhile Hal wrote stories about each trip. They purchased their famous *Whisper* in 1966 and the following year set off on a voyage through the south and western Pacific to Japan. They returned to California by sailing east across the northern Pacific via the Aleutian Islands and Alaska. This resulted in *Two On A Big Ocean* (1972) and a 16mm documentary film.

The Roths next sailed from California to Maine via Cape Horn. The book and film that followed were both titled *Two Against Cape Horn* (1978). Meanwhile Roth had brought out a well-received technical book about sailing called *After 50,000 Miles*. In 1981 the Roths set off on a four-year sailing trip around the world and told about it in *Always a Distant Anchorage* (1988).

Roth, long intrigued by solo sailing, had written a book about singlehanders called *The Longest Race* (1983). Wondering if he could do such things himself, he set off in an engineless 50-footer in the 1986–87 BOC Challenge Race and sailed around the world via the Southern Ocean. He repeated the voyage in 1990–91. The two books that resulted are *Chasing the Long Rainbow* (1990) and *Chasing the Wind* (1994). During this voyage he rounded Cape Horn for the third time.

The Roths have won many awards and honors, and Hal's books have been translated into five languages. His ninth book is *We Followed Odysseus*, based on a two-year voyage that traced the route of the ancient Greek warrior.

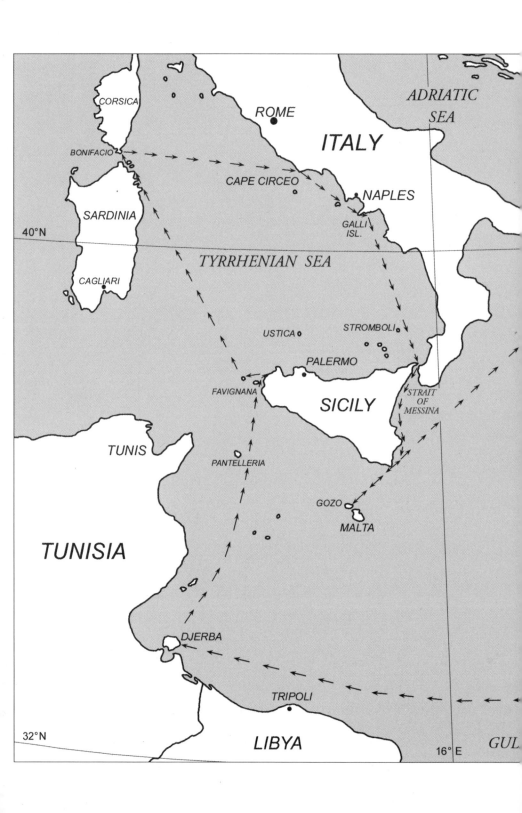